The Morning After Optimism

Methuen

1 3 5 7 9 10 8 6 4 2

First published in 1973 by The Mercier Press
Reprinted, with revisions, in *Tom Murphy Plays: 3* in 1994
by Methuen Drama

This edition published, with revisions, in 2001 by
Methuen Publishing Limited
215 Vauxhall Bridge Road,
London SW1V 1EJ

Methuen Publishing Limited Reg. No. 3543167

A CIP catalogue record for this book is available
from the British Library

ISBN 0 413 77124 5

Typeset by Wilmaset Ltd, Birkenhead, Wirral
Printed and bound in Great Britain by
Cox & Wyman Ltd, Reading, Berkshire

The Morning after Optimism

by Tom Murphy

Methuen Drama

This edition of **The Morning after Optimism** has been re-published
to coincide with the Abbey and Peacock Theatre's major season
of plays by Tom Murphy held in October 2001.

The National Theatre gratefully acknowledges the financial
support from the Arts Council/An Chomhairle Ealaíon

the arts
council
an chomhairle
ealaíon
50

The Morning after Optimism

by Tom Murphy

The Morning after Optimism by Tom Murphy opened at the Peacock Theatre on 3 October, 2001.

The play is set in a forest.

Cast

Rosie	Jasmine Russell
James	Mikel Murfi
Anastasia	Laura Murphy
Edmund	Alan Leech
Director	Gerard Stembridge
Set Designer	Bláithín Sheerin
Costume Designer	Joan O'Clery
Lighting Designer	Paul Keogan
Sound	Cormac Carroll
Stage Director	Stephen Dempsey
Assistant Stage Manager	Laura Madden
Voice Coach	Andrea Ainsworth
Festival Producer	Una Carmody
Set	Abbey Theatre Workshop
Costumes	Abbey Theatre Wardrobe Department

Tom Murphy

Plays include:

On the Outside *(w. Noel O'Donoghue)*
A Whistle in the Dark
The Orphans
A Crucial Week in the Life of a Grocer's Assistant
Famine
The Morning After Optimism
The White House
On the Inside
The Sanctuary Lamp
The J. Arthur Maginnis Story
Epitaph Under Ether *(a compilation from the works of J.M.Synge)*
The Blue Macushla
The Informer *(from the novel by Liam O'Flaherty)*
Conversations on a Homecoming
The Gigli Concert
Bailegangaire
A Thief of a Christmas
Too Late for Logic
The Patriot Game
Cupa Coffee
She Stoops to Folly *(from The Vicar of Wakefield)*
The Wake
The House

and a novel, **The Seduction of Morality**

He has received numerous awards and nominations.

Awards include: Irish Academy of Letters Award, Harveys Irish Theatre Award (twice), Sunday Tribune Arts Award, Independent Newspapers Theatre Award, Sunday Independent/Irish Life Award, Drama-Logue Critics Award, Irish Times/ESB Lifetime Award, Irish Times/ESB Theatre Award (Best Play) and Honorary Degrees from University of Dublin (Trinity College) and NUI (Galway). He was born in Tuam, County Galway. He lives in Dublin.

Gerard Stembridge *Director*

This is the first time Gerard has directed a Tom Murphy play. He did act in **The Morning After Optimism** in UCD in 1980 where he also wrote an MA thesis on Murphy's work.

Joan O'Clery *Costume Designer*

Joan's work at the Abbey and Peacock Theatres includes **Blackwater Angel, The House, The Tempest, The Wake** which toured to the Edinburgh Festival, **The Freedom of the City**, which toured to the Lincoln Center, New York and **The Colleen Bawn** which toured to the Royal National Theatre, London, **Kevin's Bed, Give Me Your Answer, Do!, A Woman of No Importance, Macbeth, The Only True History of Lizzie Finn, Philadelphia, Here I Come!, Observe the Sons of Ulster Marching Towards the Somme, Sive, The Last Apache Reunion, Rumpelstiltskin, The Third Law of Motion, Something's in the Way** and **Toupees and Snaredrums**, a CoisCéim/Abbey Theatre co-production. Joan designed the costumes for the Gate Theatre's production of **Oleanna** and was the winner of the 1997 Irish Times/ESB Costume Designer of the Year Award for her work on the Gate Theatre's **Pinter Festival**. Last year she designed the costumes for **Peer Gynt** at the Royal National Theatre, London. She also designed **Sive** by John B. Keane, Palace Theatre, Watford and Tricycle, **Licking the Marmalade Spoon**, Project Arts Centre and **Judith** at project @ the mint.

Bláithín Sheerin *Designer*

Bláithín trained in sculpture and performance art at NCAD and in theatre design at Motley @ Riverside Studios, London. Previous work at the Abbey and Peacock Theatres includes **Eden, Made in China, As the Beast Sleeps** and **You Can't Take it with You**. Other designs include **The Comedy of Errors**, RSC, **Our Father**, Almeida Theatre, **The Importance of Being Earnest**, West Yorkshire Playhouse, **Juno and the Paycock**, Lyric Theatre, **The Beckett Festival** (composite set design), Gate Theatre, John Jay Theatre, New York. She has designed for Druid, Groundwork, Charabanc, Red Kettle, TEAM, The Ark, Second Age and Prime Cut theatre companies. Her designs for Rough Magic Theatre Company include **Midden, The Whisperers, The School for Scandal, Northern Star, Pentecost, The Way of the World, The Dogs, Digging for Fire** and **Love and a Bottle**.

Paul Keogan *Lighting Designer*

Born in Dublin Paul studied Drama at the Samuel Beckett Centre, Trinity College Dublin and at Glasgow University. Paul was Production Manager for Project Arts Centre from 1994 to 1996. His designs for the Abbey and Peacock Theatres include **Melonfarmer, The Electrocution of Children, Amazing Grace, Living Quarters, Making History, The Map Maker's Sorrow, Cúirt an Mheán Oíche, Treehouses, Mrs Warren's Profession, Eden, The Tempest** and **Tartuffe**. Other work includes **Down onto Blue, Danti Dan,** Rough Magic Theatre Company, **The Silver Tassie,** Almeida Theatre, **The Gay Detective,** Project Arts Centre, **Electroshock, Quartet** and **Quay West,** Bedrock Productions, **La Bohème, L'Elisir d'Amore, The Marriage of Figaro, Madama Butterfly, Lady Macbeth of Mtsensk** and **The Silver Tassie,** Opera Ireland, **The Lighthouse,** Opera Theatre Company, **The Makropulos Case,** Opera Zuid, Netherlands, **Ballads, Seasons** and **Straight with Curves,** CoisCéim, **Sweat, Beautiful Tomorrow** and **Without Hope or Fear**, Mandance, **Territorial Claims, Chimera,** Daghdha, **SAMO,** Block & Steel, **Macalla, Intimate Gold,** Irish Modern Dance Theatre, **Angel-Babel,** Operating Theatre, **The Whiteheaded Boy,** Barabbas, **Much Ado about Nothing,** Bickerstaffe, **The Spirit of Annie Ross,** Druid Theatre Company, **The Wishing Well,** a large scale outdoor projection piece for Kilkenny Arts Festival 1999, and most recently **Too Late for Logic** by Tom Murphy, Edinburgh International Festival.

The Abbey Theatre would like to thank:

Sponsors
Aer Lingus
Anglo Irish Bank
Calouste Gubenkian Foundation
Ferndale Films
Dr. A. J. F. O'Reilly
Oman Moving & Storage
RTE
Smurfit Ireland Ltd
Viacom Outdoor
The Irish Times

Benefactors
Aer Rianta
AIB Group
An Post
Behaviour and Attitudes
eircom
Electricity Supply Board
Independent News and Media PLC
Irish Life & Permanent plc
IIB Bank
Merc Partners
John & Viola O'Connor
Pfizer International Bank Europe
Scottish Provident Ireland
SDS
SIPTU
Unilever Ireland plc
VHI

Patrons
J. G. Corry
Brian Friel
Guinness Ireland Group
Irish Actors Equity
Gerard Kelly & Co
McCullough-Mulvin Architects
Mercer Ltd
Smurfit Corrugated Cases
Sumitomo Finance (Dublin)
Total Print and Design
Francis Wintle

Sponsors of the National Theatre Archive
Jane & James O'Donoghue
Sarah & Michael O'Reilly
Rachel & Victor Treacy

Friends of the Abbey
Patricia Barnett
Mr. Ron Bolger
Ms. Patricia Brown
Ms. Ann Byrne
Mr. Joseph Byrne
Ms. Zita Byrne
Lilian & Robert Chambers
Ms. Orla Cleary
Claire Cronin
Ms. Dolores Deacon
Ms. Patricia Devlin
Karen Doull
Paul & Florence Flynn
Ms. Christina Goldrick
Mrs. Rosaleen Hardiman
Sean & Mary Holahan
Mrs. Madeleine Humphreys
Ms. Eileen Jackson
Ms. Kate Kavanagh
Mr. Francis Keenan
Mr. Peter Keenan
Vivienne & Kieran Kelly
Joan & Michael Keogh
Donal & Máire Lowry
Mr. Fechin Maher
Una M. Moran
McCann FitzGerald Solicitors
Ellie McCullough
Mr. Joseph McCullough
Marcella & Aidan McDonnell
Liam MacNamara
Dr. Chris Morash
Mr. Frank Murray
Mr. Vincent O'Doherty
Ms. Mary O'Driscoll
Mr. Dermot & Ita O'Sullivan
Mr. Andrew Parkes
Mr. Terry Patmore
Dr. Colette Pegum
Mr. Michael P. Quinn
Mr. Noel Ryan
Breda & Brendan Shortall
Fr. Frank Stafford

Personnel

The Morning After Optimism

The Morning After Optimism was first performed at The
Abbey Theatre, 15 March 1971, with the following cast:

Rosie	Eithne Dunne
James	Colin Blakely
Anastasia	Nuala Hayes
Edmund	Bryan Murray

Directed by Hugh Hunt
Designed by Bronwen Casson
Lighting by Leslie Scott

Characters

James, *a pimp, temporarily retired: his mother died recently*
Rosie, *a whore, his girl friend*
Edmund, *a young poet with an archaic gimmick*
Anastasia, *an orphan*

A forest.
Introductory and bridging music from Symponie
Fantastique (Berlioz)

Scene One

A forest. The tree-trunks reach up so high that we do not see the branches.

The cawing of a crow, then **Rosie** *and* **James** *enter.* **Rosie** *is carrying a suitcase. She stops, waits for instructions.* **James**, *unencumbered, is looking back to see if they are being followed.*

James *is middle-aged and neurotic. His spivish dress is exaggerated. A moustache. His 'evil' is self-lacerating. He races across the stage to check the opposite direction for a pursuer; after a moment he races back again and off. (His running and posing are stylised: breakneck speed, or trotting daintily, feigning cockiness; taking stances as if to say his body is a dangerous weapon; at other times his stance wilting pathetically.)*

Seeing that instructions are not forthcoming, **Rosie** *takes the initiative. She opens the suitcase and produces two stools. The suitcase is convertible and is turned into a table equipped with aluminium legs. The table and stools are a matching suite.*

Rosie *is 37. Her dress suggests a dated whore. Her catering for* **James** *is a mixture of sympathy, insecurity and malice. She takes refuge in self-deceit.*

James *returns racing through the trees, and off.*

Rosie *produces two plastic cups and a bottle of gin from her large handbag. She pours gin into each mug. She looks about, unsure as to where* **James** *is. She calls:*

Rosie Tea's up!

James *returns, his run slowing to a cocky trot. He sits tensely, ignoring his gin. The forest towering around them.* **Rosie** *sighs, feigning contentment.* **James** *winces at her effort. After a moment she tries again, hopefully conversational:*

This is a funny looking forest, James.

James (*whispering, indulging in alarm*)   What forest? Where? . . . What's funny about it?

Rosie   I don't know.

James   Then what are you talking about? (*Pause.*) Do you not like the look of it?

Rosie   Like, I'm not sure. What do you think of it?

James   I don't think anything of it! Now! I will not be made a fool of!

Pause.

Rosie   Oh, there's a little village over there –

James   Seen it, poxy village!

Rosie   Still, it's quiet.

James   Girls there dressed up in puppy-fat, I suppose.

Rosie   You put an over-emphasis on girls, James.

James   Not thro' choice.

Rosie   No, not through choice.

James   But – not – anymore. Now!

Rosie   Still, it's out of the way, what do you say? off the beaten track so to speak.

James   It would suit me to see them all as ugly as porridge.

Rosie   And perhaps we could rent a little cabin for the interim.

James   Hairy faces and turkeys' craws. What?

Rosie   As ugly as sin, James.

James   Mouths like torn pockets. Now!

Suddenly, **James** *is trotting about again to see if they are being followed*:

Bastard, 'Feathers'!

Rosie   No, we're safe, James.

James   But I've got a trick or two up my sleeve.

Rosie   That last bit of cross-country was a brilliant notion.

James   . . . Whoever he is.

Rosie   Whatever he wants, James.

James   I know he hasn't got money for me anyway. (*A grim laugh.*) A pot of gold.

Rosie   Oh, that's very funny, James. (*Going into an old routine, a sort of song and shuffle, to amuse him.*) My name is Rose-ee, Rose-ee! I'm widely known and popular! —

James (*hurtful*)   Once upon a time — once upon a time.

Rosie   Okay, once upon a time.

James (*to himself*)   Once upon a time.

Rosie   Popularity waning! —

James   Wear and tear.

Rosie   I admit it.

James   Yeh?

Rosie   I'm not too per-tic-ular-like, no more! I'm not too per-pen-dicular! No conditions! —

James   One condition (*Money.*)

Rosie   Only one condition. (*New material.*) My brains are danced on like grapes to make abortions!

He laughs. She is pleased.

I say my head is sore! (*They laugh.*)
My belly is a tub of moss! (*They laugh.*)
Yo-ho-ho and the tits are for whom!

The laughter subsiding.

James   I've been everybody's victim for too long.

Rosie   Far too long – Tell us a really filthy story, James.

James   Magic-mirror-on-the-wall, who is the fairest of them all!

They laugh again.

I'll tell you a story.

Rosie   Yes. (*She has heard it before.*)

James   I'm standing on my usual corner –

Rosie   A Monday night –

James   A Monday night, business is bad, I'm about to go home and enjoin you myself.

Rosie   A wind comes up.

James   A newspaper billowing, coming round the corners, deserting a lamp-post to wrap itself around my ankles. Now, what is the thought in my mind as I bend to unravel those sheets?

Rosie   Blue knickers.

James   Adolescent blue knickers. And the thought persists as I read 'Come home, mother dead, foreign papers please copy'. Do you see my point?

Rosie   The item trimmed in black meant nothing.

James   Nothing. And I said to myself, you've come a long way, Jimmy kid. And I said to myself, I like it. I couldn't care less about my mammy. Now! (*Intensely.*) And to her dead hand, so mottled brown, so worn with care, steals nightly in my bed, (*He brushes his hand across his face.*) I say, nickerdehpazzee!

Rosie (*mechanically*)   Nickerdehpazzee, James.

James (*to himself*)   Now.

Rosie   But what do you say to a little cabin for the interim?

James (*to himself*)   Yeh know.

Rosie (*to herself*)   What is your suggestion, I feel so guilty, once upon a time I knew the name of every single bird.

James   But could you recognise them?

Rosie   I could.

James   Well, it would suit me if someone came along and stabbed the lot of them.

Rosie   Once I knew every flower.

James   And everyone knows they are covered in fleas.

In the background, **Anastasia** *entering: glimpses of her walking through the trees, a water urn in her hand. She is a beautiful barefooted girl of about seventeen, her dress ragged in the most becoming way. She does not see them: they do not see her. She exits.*

Rosie   Yes. I think you should just sit right down and have a good cry. For yourself. You feel the better for it, they say. Grief is bad at the best of times. Give vent to it. Cry to lose it. And there's nothing to be ashamed of in the male tear. And it might be cheaper on your nerves, and on mine, in the long run. And take consolation: you have tolerable earning potential (*Herself.*) and you're not finished yet. Not by a long chalk. Why properly pruned of the dead wood you could be almost anything. You could almost be yourself. And then say, *non, je ne regrette rien*, no I will have no regrets. And *che sera, sera*, if you like. And then get on with the business of living. In any case that's what I did. And I feel the better for it.

James (*grimly*)   Can't say two kind words to me.

Rosie (*absently, softly*)   Otherwise it will crucify you.

James   Can you?

Rosie   Yes. I know of a person who, when she found out that things are really what they seem and not what they are supposed to be, instead of manifesting her reaction in a little tear, held back and clung to her pain. Until, one day, as she was silently hanging out the washing on the line, a gander came hissing from the end of the garden, chasing her indoors. Then she cried. She nearly died. But too late. To this day that woman believes she is a goose.

James   You want to see me crying, don't you? Well, you won't! You or anybody else. I've had enough! You don't know what's on my mind now, do you?

Rosie (*fears he is thinking of leaving her*)   We've been together a long time, James.

James   What's that got to do with it? I'm waiting here for 'Feathers'!

He trots about.

Rosie   No, we're safe!

James   No, we're not. (*Triumphantly.*) I left a trail for him to follow!

Rosie (*considers*)   . . . Yes. Wait for him, see who he is, what he wants, have it out. Let's have done with him.

James   I've got a trick or two. Up my sleeve. (*Now feebly, nervously.*)

Rosie   Since you're not afraid of him, you said.

James   He's following you too.

Rosie   Oh no, he's not, James.

James (*his frustration and anger overcome his fear*)
Everybody's victim! Well, not anymore! Those puppy-fat princesses! No more! And that feathered bastard shadowing me – a Monster! I'll stop him in his tracks. And that night rambling corpse of a mammy! I'll lay that dead

witch sleeping! (*To* **Rosie**.) Go! *Rent* that cabin! (*He strikes a fighting pose.*) Yes, you're coming of age at last. Well, come on, come on, dragon-feathers, try me! Just don with pride that honest evil mantle tried and true for this great task, Jimmy kid, and you can't lose. Keep your evil wits, don't go balloon, and do not deviate.

Rosie *has packed the suitcase. He shouts at her.*

Go!

Rosie *exits.*

James' *stance wilting.*

Yeh know . . . Once I saw a girl, her back in headscarf and raincoat, once. I just passed by, I didn't see her face, in my blue motorcar, and turned left for Eros and the statue of Liberty, and became ponce in the graveyard. She may have been Miss Right, she certainly was Miss Possible, cause my hidden, real, beautiful self manifested itself in a twinge . . . Just to hold her hand, yeh know.

Anastasia *enters background, playfully carrying the water urn on her head.*

James, *unobserved by her, gaping at her. Then angry because 'Feathers' has not showed up, leaving him available for this temptation.*

Feathers! Feathers!

Anastasia *exits.*

James *starts to follow, at first reluctantly, then racing, taking a wide circle to intercept her.*

The lights are fading.

Edmund *is entering, not clearly defined: a tall figure wearing a feathered Robin Hood hat.*

Scene Two

Patches of light and shade in the forest. **Anastasia** *running in circles, in fear. Off, the roars of anonymous wild animals.*

Then **James**, *off and as he enters, shouting, as if driving away the animals.*

James. Yaa hah-haa hah-haa! Yaa hah-haa, hah-haa!

James *trotting towards her, unsure, smiling against his face.*

I got rid of them, rid of them, dangerous, they're gone, unfamiliar, away, now . . . Saved you, rescued, I mean, rescued, rescued, so I'm glad you were not drowning or anything like that. For I am a poor swimmer, yeh know . . . But, that's that. (*About to leave.*)

Anastasia   What were they?

James   What – what?

Anastasia   My heart! What species?

James   Oh!

Anastasia   I have not heard of animals so wild in this forest before.

James   No gregarious cats were they, hah-hah!

Anastasia   The shock!

James   Yes.

Anastasia   I'm grateful. (*She smiles.*)

James   Yes! I mean, one of them, one of them nearly, one of them nearly bit the-the (*hand*) off me . . . But the danger's past, so Jimmy can go now, and dealt with. (*She puts down the urn.*) That's a very nice jug.

Anastasia   Thank you.

James   What? And – not at all – And – Oh, you're lovely! (*A step towards her; he pulls himself up.*) I meant –

Anastasia   Thank you.

James   What? (*Delighted.*) I mean – You are! I meant
that! You're all that! And more! Not a smelly hippy. I
suspect we've got the same values. There's an overall style
about you. I ask you, style? Maxi, mini, one or the other,
but the two of them together? don't make me laugh.
Twelve inches of provocative thigh, laid bare, fleeting
glimpses, under a cold long Russian overcoat! What for?
Just to be chased, laid waste – Do you see what I mean?
Nothing lofty. Even so, where does it get the hopeful
chaser? Drop dead. I don't speak the same language, see?
Or if I do and click, it's lay-me-down-I'm-a-dead-mutton-
chick! No conversation. Nor worth the winning. Some day
my prince will come? Don't make me laugh – they make
me puke! – they do nothing for me! I walk away and I say,
thank you for the comparison. The whip I'd give them.
No, not for Jimmy here. My mother told me to look for a
bit of decorum. She used to play piano – (*Miming pianist.*)
With her hands – Unblemished then – Nickerdehpazzee!
But she would like your style and I certainly like your
spirit. Yes, I must confess I do, and I've been twice round
the world and not by boat, which brings me to the point I
wanted to make. Ah . . . (*He has forgotten the point.*)
Nevertheless, what's your name, yeh know?

Anastasia (*girlishly playful*)   You don't know?

James   Should I?

Anastasia   No.

James   What?

Anastasia   Guess.

James   Ah –

Anastasia   Yes.

James   What?

Anastasia (*spelling*)   A. N. A –

James   Ann!

Anastasia   No. S. T. A. S. I. A.

James   . . . Anastasia! (*An impetuous step towards her, pulls himself up. Then a deliberate step away, from her.*) See? (*A trot taking him further away from her.*) See? (*She does not understand.*) . . . Rushing things. We must be careful. My father vas a Russian, my mother vas a Russian, but I, I take my time! Joke. (*She starts giggling.*) Me for you, and you for me, and tea for two and hah-hah-hah! (*He considers dancing with her, changes his mind, dances with the urn.*) A fellow and a girl in a dance hall, see? and he says to her 'Some dance!' and she says to him 'Some don't.' (*He pauses for a moment, melting at her smiling innocence. Tongue-tied.*) Ana-Ana-Ana. (*Her smile disappears, a moment of fear. He starts to dance again.*) 'It's a lovely floor' he said to her 'Why don't you dance on it?' she said to him.

He puts the urn on the ground behind him. The slightest suggestion that the urn is a hostage.

Why don't you dance on it, it's a very nice jug. Now, you might think me outspoken, but I like to think I'm direct. I like to think of a clean slate, yeh know. Why? You well may ask. As a basis for a proper little proposition. So, to come to the point, I'm coming to, Ana-Ana-Ana, a new chance is all I want. Hmm?

She giggles. He wipes his brow.

No, Ana-Ana-Ana, serious.

Anastasia   Sorry?

James   Holidays?

Anastasia   I live here.

James   I guessed that. Don't for a moment think I didn't. But I didn't want to ask were you a *native*. It might be considered a coarse word. But now, nevertheless, what I mean to say, yeh know, is, so, what do you say to that?

Anastasia   I'm an orphan.

James   Aaa.

Anastasia   I've been alone for some time and long to be found.

James   I am very lonely too. And there is no other?

Anastasia   Not as yet.

James   We have an awful lot in common.

Anastasia (*smiles*)   Yes.

James   What?

Anastasia   Yes.

James   And I'm free! Totally free!

Anastasia   But do not misunderstand –

James   See how easy it is to talk to me?

Anastasia } But do not –
James   } Shh, and listen! . . . Didn't you hear a
                solitary bird sing over there just now?

Anastasia   A what?

James   An omen. I don't really dislike the birds. Yeh know. Not when I'm happy. I have nice thoughts, see. I wouldn't stab them. The crow is my friend. It's nice to run one's fingers through one's hair, hmm? It's nice to run one's fingers through your hair, hmm? Let me run my fingers through your hair only?

Anastasia   What nonsense!

James (*staggered*)   What – what? A fella and a girl in a dance hall, see, and –

Anastasia (*nervously*)   You are being foolish.

James   No I'm not. If you're worried about – about, well, I won't. Not without your consent – Not at all! But before you speak, Ana-Ana-Ana, have to play it fair, want to play it straight, cause today is now or never – Would you like to hear the story of my life? I'll erase it as I talk, for the slate, clean slate, tabula rasa or caput. I've known the bluest score, I've had the biggest ball, but don't jump to conclusions, no don't make me laugh, never irretrievably lost, yeh know . . . The permissive society? I was a member, when that club was exclusive, when 'twas dangerous to be in it, when the tension was there. And I might have got lost, but they threw open the doors, didn't they? The amateurs came in to desecrate with innocence; everybody in, doing it with flowers; the pros were in despair, the cons were in confusion – Pollen, pollen everywhere! – There was too much of it about to go around! Do you see what I mean? I uttered a prayer, Jesus, Mary and Joseph, where is the sin any more, I said! . . . Irretrievably – irretrievably lost never . . . So, shacked up with Rosie, tried to figure it all out, but something had depressed me, took to looking at the ceiling, and while wrestling with morality, put Rosie on the game. (*Reflective*.) Yeh know . . . And I could have expanded. I could have been the very best. Why, they napped *me* to be the berries in my trade! But that was me always: Played it along with the single cow – Why? You well may ask *again* – when I could have had twenty top-notch harlots in my stall. I'll tell you why, I've just worked it all out! I was practising *monogomy* for when the real thing came along. As promised. See, I've thought of you a lot. Anastasia was the name whispered by the wind. Hmm? (*She looks frightened for a moment*.) Oh, but do not get me wrong, it was not that straight and narrow, and we agreed the cleanest slate for our little proposition: I tell all . . . If you had seen me, on the quiet, having my slice, on any old side, with any old whore, you'd have called me Ping-Pong: From Biddy to Jackie, scrubber to moohair, penthouse to doorway – pickpocketing their pennies while engaged in the act! But that was me always, never committed: Those sorties were swift. Well, the wind would start whispering, Hans Christian Anderson, (and) I'd go back to my base, for another session with the ceiling, always descending, the walls closing in, and my ideals always, my ideals always,

my ideals always, suffering insomnia! And here I am. As
you can very well see. But today, I am glad I kept my
ideals. Oh, have no doubts about that. And as from now,
I've forgotten everything I know. And now I would like, I
would like, I would like, I would like to combine with your
sweet self from scratch. Hmmm?

Anastasia   I must go now.

She starts to move to retrieve the urn. **James** *lunges instinctively to
stop her.* **Anastasia** *is terrified.* **James** *is horrified that they have
reached this impasse.*

James   No, I can make you happy, I can make you
laugh! –

Anastasia   No! No! –

James   We had some laughs, remember? My father vas
a –

Anastasia   No! No! –

James   Look what's this, what's this? (*He is imitating a
hen.*)

Anastasia   Though I am orphaned in this world –

James   A hen, a hen!

Anastasia   Do not think that any farmyard plan of
yours –

James   What's this, what's this? (*The sounds of the
anonymous wild animals that we heard at the start of the scene. He
realises his mistake.*)

Anastasia   . . . Can frighten or –

James   That was not to frighten you! –

Anastasia   Distort the picture of my hope –

James   An innocent way of getting to meet you!

Anastasia   For I have dreamed of one who'll come to
these woods and find me –

James   No good to me by intimidation!

Anastasia   A man with eyes flaming green –

James   No good to me by force!

Anastasia   Burning equally for righteousness and love for me –

James   I'm prepared to tie my feet together! –

Anastasia   His shining purest youth. Being acknowledged even by the grass that loves his tread –

James   Don't keep thinking about sex!

Anastasia   So slender, so certain, so perfect –

James   I consider it a secondary thing –

Anastasia   So tall.

James (*his head rolling in confusion*)   A secondary thing – a secondary thing! Had I considered it a primerary thing – a primerary thing, at the top of my profession! Where are the old values? – What about the promises? Not that I asked the questions willingly. But voices from the past, my ideals always, bogged down upon the fairy-tale! Let me be frank, I'm not complaining – I am complaining – I'd like to know, one way or the other that there is or is not, something more than the momentary pleasure . . . My very last try, or I'm afraid I must end it all and find my feet, Anastasia . . . I'm saying your eyes are blue, your hair is long, your skin is whiter than ever I was told.

Anastasia's *hand sloping towards the urn. Without looking up,* **James** *puts his hand inside his jacket, withdraws a knife.* **Anastasia** *is still.*

I was hoping, by your presence, that my hidden real beautiful self would, yeh know, show itself. I'm very beautiful, yeh know, but it's in hiding or something. And I'd like to feel its twinge once more . . . A try?

Anastasia.   No.

James   We're alone.

Anastasia   No.

James   And could start here, the two of us.

Anastasia   I must go now.

Slowly, fearfully, she starts to walk away. **James**, *motionless knife in hand.*

James   Come 'ere a minute . . . Come 'ere a minute.

Suddenly she dashes off.
A moment's pause and he is dashing after her.
Rosie *enters hauling a cylinder of gas.*

Rosie   James! I've rented the most secluded little cabin.

James (*rounds on her*)   Strumpet, slut, whore, Rosie!

He exits.

Rosie   I only wanted to tell you where the cabin is.
(*Delayed action.*) Pimp, ponce, Jame-Jame! (*Then tearfully.*)
I'll get you, Jame-Jame . . .

And suddenly she freezes. **Edmund** *is entering. He is a handsome, confident young man in his early twenties. He is very innocent, romantic and charming. He wears a Robin Hood hat with a feather, an antique military tunic, jeans, high boots, a sword and a water-flask at his side.*

He alters his course and exits without seeing her.

'Feathers'! What an escape! I was sure he would nab me. A Monster! Strong looking. Striking. My heart, if he had caught me! Or is he playing King Cagey? He wouldn't just ignore me?

She collects her cylinder of gas and exits, following him.

Hello there! . . . Hello there!

Scene Three

Another part of the forest.

Anastasia's *urn placed conspicuously on the ground.* **Anastasia** *enters tearfully. She sees the urn and hurries towards it joyfully. Her hand on the urn, and simultaneously* **James** *steps out from behind a tree, triumphantly. He has his knife in one hand: he takes her hand and she appears submissive as he starts to lead her away. She stops. He looks at her suspiciously. Suddenly, she starts to scream, which he has not anticipated.* **James** *in consternation.*

James. Shush! shush!

Edmund (*off*)   Hullo-a! Hullo-a!

James   'Feathers'! – 'Feathers'!

Edmund (*off*)   Hullo-a! –

Rosie (*off*)   Hello there! –

James   Shush, please shush!

In the struggle **Anastasia** *cuts her finger on* **James**' *knife. She holds up her injured finger and faints.* **Edmund** *enters background, criss-crossing through the trees, searching for the source of the screams.* **James** *watching* **Edmund** *working his way closer.*

Edmund   Hullo-a!

James   But don't I know those features?

There is not time to carry off **Anastasia**; **James** *hides behind a tree or climbs up into the tree.*

Edmund   Hullo-a!

Rosie (*entering background*)   Hello there!

Through the scene **Rosie** *works her way forward gradually, hauling cylinder of gas.*

Edmund *finds* **Anastasia** *and for a moment he fears the worst. He revives her with a kiss. They look at each other in wonder.*

Edmund   . . . But who are you?

Anastasia   Anastasia.

Edmund   Anastasia!

Anastasia   And your eyes, green!

Edmund   Anastasia!

Anastasia   Can it be?

Edmund   Edmund is my name.

Anastasia   Edmund!

Edmund   Anastasia! . . . But the way I found you here? Your hand: Is it not a knife wound?

Anastasia   From the blade of a dark horse who lay in wait, his red eye rolling in a starvation he claimed I could fill. How you must have come in the nick of time!

Edmund   But what if beast still lurks here, hiding in the thickets.

Anastasia   Would he dare now that you are here.

Edmund   Nevertheless. (*Wisely.*) I begin to learn a thing or two in travelling, you know.

Anastasia   And I pleaded with him.

Edmund   Yes?

Anastasia   But he closed his ears with monkey sounds.

Edmund   And then?

Anastasia   We struggled.

Edmund   He did not?

Anastasia   No.

Edmund   Twas good, twas good, twas good, indeed, for I've been told that in the woe of such an act, the brightest gold of female spirit turns to brass contaminate.

Anastasia   And your voice a poet's.

Edmund   All changed.

Anastasia *nods.*

Edmund   Changed utterly. So now I must find two men.
But let me bind this wicked wound. (*He binds her hand with
his cravat.*)

Anastasia   You came in search of a *man*?

Edmund   My brother James who has been long lost. Of
his appearance my memory is vague for he still had years
to grow a man when he left home. And through thrice nine
lands I've wandered, being misued and mocked by words I
did not understand. Once I journeyed North to find there
was a James, but long gone 'poling'? wanderlusted South.
And to a land down under where they told me of a last-
remembered prisoned James, accused of rifling 'boxes' of
the poor and convicted of the same offence 'gainst convent
postulants.

Anastasia (*uncomprehending wonder*)   Oh.

Edmund   In a vineless place there lived a drunkard
James. In another and another, a pretender and imposter
who'd present to me assuméd christian name and face, two
pots of legacy-expectancy for eyes.

Anastasia   Oh.

Edmund   And even in that parish last of all, where the
aura was forbearance and the tenor fortitude, and I
thought, at last, this is the end, for those attributes would
compliment the standards of my brother: There I did, with
galloping optimism of results, ignore the minor signposts,
and straightaway the very top did go to his most serene the
smiling red-haired bishop. His rosy ruby ring I kissed –
And gold crozier as well – They well set off his smock and
hat, a most imposing cleric's drag! But scarce my
genuflecting ritual was done and I had spoken of my quest,
than at mention of the name of James, the red-haired
bishop's smiling face went tighting into august ire, his holy
head did copper-beach, and summoned by the bells that

pealed emergency in Roman morse, two military P.P.s arrived to lead me to the shore and feed me to an oarless boat. And here I am.

Anastasia   My poor brave love.

Edmund   But when we meet the noble evidence of James will show as candle does when lighted under tinder bush.

James, *sloping away, steps on a twig – or he nearly falls out of the tree.*

Anastasia   Oh, what was that?

They are poised listening, **Edmund** *hand on sword.*

Edmund   A crow.

Anastasia   A crow?

Edmund   The only bird I loathe!

Other twigs snapping.

Anastasia   And that!

Edmund   And that! –

Rosie (*approaching, steps on a twig, calls softly*)   Hello there! –

Anastasia   And that! –

Rosie *has just seen* **Edmund** *and she is pleased with herself. (Neither* **Edmund** *nor* **Anastasia** *see her.) Then her terror as* **Edmund** *speaks angrily, drawing his sword.*

Edmund (*drawing sword*)   Tis the bane! No loathed crow could make such noise!

Rosie *bolts for it. The noise she makes running through the trees confuses* **Edmund** *and he alters his course to follow her.*

He thinks to escape! Now I shall accomplish half the remainder of my mission!

Anastasia *watches* **Edmund** *rush off, admiring his manly courage and anger.*

James *returns and grabs her – or he drops off the tree and lands beside her.*

James Didn't want to meet you, puppy-fat, did I? Had sworn never-more.

Anastasia Ed–

James (*twisting her arm*) Go on, try shouting again now, go on.

He tears a piece of cloth off her dress and throws it on the path opposite the one he intends to take.

Anastasia Edmund will find me.

James (*bitterly*) Edmund. I should have known. Well, it only makes it worse who he is!

Anastasia Where are you taking me?

James I'll find a place. This time I leave no trail.

Edmund *is returning.* **James** *hurries off with* **Anastasia**.

Edmund He escaped this time, but my promise to thrash him will be . . . Anastasia? (*Calls.*) Anastasia, where are you?

Rosie *enters background, ready to run again, a mixture of terror and delight, breathing heavily.* **Rosie** *comes forward cautiously.*

Rosie Hello there!

Edmund Anastasiaaa! (*To himself.*) If needs be I shall do that villain in, you know?

Rosie (*striking whore's pose*) Can I help you?

Edmund (*striding past* **Rosie** *to pick up the piece of cloth torn off* **Anastasia**'s *dress*) Ah! God directs my steps. (*He is about to exit.*)

Rosie (*angry at being ignored*) Whom do you bloody-well think you're following, Feathers?

Edmund *turns about and draws his sword.* **Rosie** *sinks to her knees, trying to protect her head and ribs with her arms. Then* **Edmund** *strides past her and kills a snake.*

Edmund   Oh, that you were the villain, snake!

Rosie *faints,* **Edmund** *revives her, slapping her hands.*

Maybe with her wits a little fostered she could help me.

Rosie   Oh my love, I love you so much.

Edmund   There is beauty in the blue truth of your eye and your eye is not light, I cannot be thine.

Rosie   It was just a salutation.

Edmund   And you are fairer than anyone knows at a second glance.

Rosie   Forget it.

Edmund   Someone can help you.

Rosie   Little Jesus.

Edmund   He has graced you with sensitivity.

Rosie (*loudly, cynically*)   And my legs! You noticed my feelings, but not bad, are they? (*She has pulled up her skirt.*) What's your game?

Edmund   I had hoped for information of the maiden Anastasia.

Rosie   The one with the jug on her head?

Edmund   You know her!

Rosie   I was looking for a cylinder of gas for the cabin.

Edmund   Yes, yes – yes?

Rosie   She gave me directions, that's all.

Edmund   She is fair, she is lovely.

Rosie   She's a wet kid, she knows nothing!

Edmund   She is —

Rosie   Nothing! (**Rosie** *is quietly triumphant at killing the subject.*)

Edmund (*moving off*)   She cannot help me.

Rosie   Hold on! I mean, people get the wrong idea if we girls make too much of other girls, get me? Better to stick to the traditional stuff: meeow! Okay?

Edmund (*does not understand*)   Yes.

Rosie (*watching his face*)   I like your boots . . . And your water-flask. Oh, and ostrich, is it? Very nice. (**Edmund** *feels flattered.*) Hmm? I mean, you didn't come here trailing the kid now, did you?

Edmund   But our paths have been converging since the exordium.

Rosie   The things you boys say to me! Honestly! The way you boys will cling to the crap! Man is a fool, they say. Me now, I shed tears and crap, all in one go; I don't get involved, not any more, my name is Rosie, and I feel the better for it . . . You don't believe me? Well, alright, I confess. One single dream remaining. But adult, practical and possible. For I have dreamed, you see, that someone someday'd come along and turn my working blanket into a magic carpet. Away! Just once will be enough. (*She smiles at him.*) My real name is Mary Rose. Unsolicited, persons started to call me Rosie.

Edmund   Then I shall call you Mary Rose.

Rosie   Do you kiss?

Edmund   Mary Rose —

Rosie   You don't have to get involved —

Edmund   But the maiden Anastasia.

Rosie   She'd be no use to you! Tck! He doesn't understand.

Edmund (*wisely*)   Oh, I know a thing or two.

Rosie   Yeh? . . . I'm beginning to see you're pretty sharp alright. And maybe my little dream remaining is near fulfilment. I'll help you.

Edmund   I'll pay you.

Rosie *flicks out her hand for him to kiss it.*

Rosie   For a start.

Edmund   Mary Rose –

Rosie   Kiss my hand –

Edmund   Believe you must –

Rosie   It's just a hand –

Edmund   That fidelity's single breach –

Rosie   You saved my life –

Edmund   Would me impossible make for Anastasia.

Rosie   My platonic poxy hand, for little Jesus' sake!

As he kisses her hand.

Got him . . . Now, what's your game?

Edmund   I am now in search of three.

Rosie   And the second you seek?

Edmund   A villain.

Rosie   Yes James, and – (*Her hand to her mouth, fears she has made a slip.*)

Edmund   You know James? The third I seek is James!

Rosie   Well, he's just a friend, a kind of sort of Bill.

Edmund (*about to exit*)   She cannot help me or herself.

Rosie   I'll lead you to James!

He stops.

Well, you'll give him no more than a right good belting,
right? (*Angrily*.) Well, the fact is, I need spectacles. What
ammunition the ponce would make of that if he knew! And
what ammunition for me if I'm forced to return and go my
profession alone wearing spectacles!

Edmund (*to himself*)   This does not sound a likely James.

Rosie   What? Well, do you know – Do-you-know! – that
every single day in nineteen years he's thought of ditching
me, leaving me? Do you know that? He would too, but he
thinks I'd die without him.

Edmund   And would you not?

Rosie   No.

Edmund   That's the pity.

Rosie (*softly*)   I know. (*Shakes off the sadness*.) No need for
your jaws to grow long with sincerity about it!

Edmund   But what are his accomplishments?

Rosie   His mother played piano.

Edmund   What?!

Rosie   And do you know that, in spite of all, I appear to
cater for his every whim? Do you know that? But the fact
that I appear to cater for his every whim means nothing.
The truth is in the opposite, they say. I'll lead you to him.
Spiritually we have nothing. Except the poxy habit of
time. And ask myself to recall when his intimacies meant
other than a client's, and my memory only shrugs and
shakes its head.

Edmund (*his mother*)   Played piano?

Rosie   Yes! My daddy and my uncle Joe were right:
What do I know of the ponce!

Edmund   Concert?

Rosie   Exactly! Concert? Honky-tonk? One hand?

They exit with cylinder of gas.

Scene Four

A log cabin in the forest. (For this scene the cabin retains its fourth wall: we do not see **Anastasia**.) **James** *comes out of cabin. He calls back.*

James   But latent sexuality can thicken the air unduly. So, to come to the point I'm coming to, I'm not saying we should preclude irrevocably what could become pleasure at some later date. (*To himself.*) A stroke of luck finding this place alright. Secluded. Safe. That stupid dumb-cluck Rosie's probably rented a little cabin right in among the dirty natives.

Rosie (*off*)   This way! The thing is he mightn't be at home.

James, *in consternation, in and out of the cabin, and in again.*

Rosie *and* **Edmund** *entering.*

(*Points to the cabin.*) Isn't it nice? (*Calls.*) James! He's not at home. But let me show you what it's like inside.

James *comes out of the cabin. Trying to conceal his fear, holding the door closed behind him. He is now wearing a pair of dark glasses.* **Rosie**'s *surprise and disappointment. She goes forward.*

How did you find it?

James   Aw Jesus! (*Quietly.*) Get the bastard out of here.

Rosie   Stall it, relax, the kid's a mug.

James   Aw Jesus! (*Loudly.*) Where have you been, madam?

Rosie   It's okay, we misjudged him.

James (*loudly*)   What have you been doing, madam?

Rosie   On the way here he told me he's looking for his brother or something.

James (*loudly*)   I hope you're not deaf, madam!

Rosie (*loudly, angrily*)   I-was-getting-a-cylinder-of-gas!
(*Motioning* **Edmund** *to join them.*) This is James; James, this
is – Oh, what's your name?

Edmund   My name is Edmund –

James (*ignores* **Edmund**'*s hand*)   I'll teach you to talk to
strangers!

Rosie (*angrily*)   I said I've checked him out!

James   Wait till I get you inside, madam!

Rosie   What's the big deal for? Well this is good, this is
rich, this is really bingo! He, Edmund! – Him, Edmund! –
That! – has me out on the bye-ways every night 'cept
Mondays, and now he's asking what I was doing.

James' *hand raised to strike* **Rosie**, **Edmund** *grabs his hand
and yanks him about.* **James**' *dark glasses fall off.* **Edmund**'*s
and* **James**' *heads close together, looking into each others' eyes.*
Edmund *beginning to look troubled.* **James** *growing cocky,
fancying himself, seeing* **Edmund**'*s distress. Their hands
continue, locked together, straining with each other.*

Edmund   Quickly, who are you?

Rosie   Croak him, Edmund!

James (*cockily to* **Rosie**) Who's the gomey?

Rosie   Break his arm off.

James   Who's the buffer with the archaic gimmick?

Edmund   It were better that you told me.

James   A pop-poet!

Edmund   Or I shall – I shall break your arm off!

Rosie   Do! Do!

James   Are you able? Alrighty! Let's see. Come on, good
old devil.

The contest begins in earnest, the effort, forcing them into intricate bodily contortions. **James** *is delighted, showing slightly to advantage.*

Rosie (*to* **Edmund**) Get him in the cobblers, Edmund. (*Tugging at* **James**, *feigning concern for* **James**.) Don't, James, he'll hurt you. He'll break your arm off.

James   Back, madam! Don't weaken me. I've got the bastard now.

Edmund *increases his effort and* **James** *is eventually forced to submit.*

Edmund   Do you still challenge?

James   I do! I do!

Edmund   Do you still?

James   I yi – yi – yi do!

Edmund   Still challenge?

James   I yi – yi – yi – yi! – No! I don't!

Edmund *releases him.* **James** *trots away, stops.*

I do! I do!

James *turns to run away again, trips, falls.*

Edmund (*offering his hand*)   My name is –

James   Don't want to know you, or anything to do with you! (*Stands. To* **Rosie**.) And, you! Inside! – Home! – At once!

Rosie (*pitying* **Edmund** *who looks upset*)   Aaaaa!

James   At once!

Rosie *is moving towards the cabin when* **James** *remembers that* **Anastasia** *is in there.*

Just a moment, madam!

Rosie *obeys, waits for instructions*. **James** *stuck for a reason to give her*.

Nevertheless, so, yeh know, but, well! Well, I would have won only for you! You weakened me!

Rosie   Aaa, he isn't even half wide, James, he's nice.

Edmund (*to himself*)   Something's gone awry. All others in his category did frantically claim relationship with guile. And his mother played piano.

Rosie   Aa, what's troubling you, Edmund?

James (*nervously*)   Nothing troubling me – nothing troubling me.

Edmund   A favour?

Rosie   Anything.

Edmund   I ask it simply: what is your surname?

Rosie   Well, like, mine is still sort of different, but his is –

James (*To* **Rosie**)   You stall your jills. (*To* **Edmund**.) Jones.

Edmund (*doubtfully*)   Your surname?

James   Well, what's yours?

Edmund   Oh, I have learned a thing or two in travelling, you know.

James   And I've got a trick or two myself.

Edmund   And I've evolved a formula for 'vincing truth!

James *crouches suddenly, poised, waiting for this next contest. They start to circle each other. Then suddenly.*

The old apple tree?

James   N-N-Name of a pub!

Edmund   No – In the garden.

James   On the river the one I know!

Edmund   Home, James?

James   And don't spare the horses!

Edmund (*growing dismayed*)   Teddy-bear with one ear is living in the attic.

James   Teddy Bear is a retired boxer!

James *is giggling nervously, feeling he has won.*

Edmund (*dismayed*)   . . . Bapu.

James' *giggling triumph changing to puzzlement. Then feigning casualness.*

James   Bapu?

Edmund   Twas Jameses charming infant word when asking for an apple.

The shadow of a memory on **James**' *face, his vigilance relaxing, his stance wilting and* **Edmund** *is in;* **James** *frustrated.*

Had you a very unhappy childhood, where were you born?

James   I – yi – yi – yi – Which of them?

Edmund   Place of birth.

James   I – yi – yi – yi – In a ball-alley! I was born in a –

Edmund   Your parents?

James   Were called Jones too!

Edmund   I mean, sir –

James   They were awful! – They were awful! – They were – Stop!

Edmund *is watching him with interest.*

(*Quietly.*) You'd better go home, sonny, leave us alone, sonny, go 'way, go home, people are dying.

Edmund   I will find my brother first.

James   Not here.

Edmund   I have travelled far and wide –

James   Don't want to know.

Edmund   I don't believe you are a wicked man, James
Jones –

James (*feebly*)   No baits, don't throw any baits.

Edmund   You would think that all the Jameses in the
world accursed, but I know better. I shall always know
better.

Pause. The three of them motionless. **James** *trying to maintain a
hard expression. He turns his back.* **Rosie** *comes out of her
stillness, a girlish glow about her.*

Rosie   Let's . . . Let's all do something! The three of us. I
know! The pub! A few drinks! And you can continue your
search on the way, Edmund. Do let's!

Edmund *looks at* **James**.

James *nods to them to go on ahead of him.* **Rosie** *and* **Edmund**
exit. **James** *turns about. His face easing into a weary softness.*

James   'Bapu' . . . Ah, this won't last, this feeling won't.
It's all treachery.

After a moment he breaks into a weary trot and exits following
Edmund *and* **Rosie**.

Scene Five

Night. The cabin.

Rosie, **Edmund** *and* **James** *enter, approaching the cabin.*
Rosie *and* **James** *are drunk.* **Rosie** *has a bottle of gin. They
are singing and dancing their way home.* **Edmund** *is enjoying
himself, his youthful exuberance encouraging him to complement
some of* **Rosie**'s *movements – though he does not quite partner
her.*

And though **James** *is drunk, smiling, nodding encouragingly, bringing up the rear, he is too watchful, the smile too fixed, the nodding too benign. And he is carrying* **Edmund**'s *sword, ostensibly to allow* **Edmund** *greater freedom of movement. Through the song he slips away from them, races into the cabin and hides the sword under the bed. It is mainly* **Rosie** *who does the singing; the others complement.*

Rosie (*singing*)

Life's no bucking bron-co!
How's your uncle's bald head?
Life is no dud, oh no!
Life is so good, yeah, yeah!

Come on, you old pair of pub-crawling bums! Let's have a party!

Life's no bucking bron-co! – Where's James?
Let go the bloody handlebars!
Up she flew-wuw, touché!
Life's a good screw, yeah-yeah!

The lights come up on the cabin as they enter. There is a main room which contains a few simple chairs, a table and a bed. And separated from this by a locked door is a small room on an elevated level. In the small room we see **Anastasia** *gagged and bound to a chair. She remains thus throughout the scene.*

James   Glasses, Rosie!

Rosie   Coming up, James!

James   Not bad, is she? Getting old now, but not bad, is she?

Edmund   I have great admiration for Mary Rose.

James   Hear that, Rose?

Rosie   Yep!

James (*confidentially to* **Edmund**) You wouldn't think it, but she's not a whore at all, yeh know. And she was very well educated, her father a judge and her Uncle Joe a bishop. So, I could have done worse, hmm?

Edmund   And her hospitality.

James   Yes, her hospitality – but I've done pretty well for myself when you think of it another way. I didn't make many mistakes and I –

Edmund   And her vigour.

James   Yes, yes, her vigour, her figure, but *I*, all-in-all, did alright, and I must say I –

Edmund   The pith of vigour.

James (**Edmund**'s *innocence hurting him. Harshly*)   Yes – yes, randy, boy, randy!

Edmund (*smiling*)   Yes.

James *is sulking.*

Rosie *is bringing glasses to the table.*

Rosie   Come on, Edmund, sit down. And I'll buy you a leather jock-strap trimmed with sequins tomorrow! (*Quietly.*) Stay the night. (*Loudly.*) God, that last place we were in, James, bored the knickers off me! (**James** *sighs.*) Now, Edmund, you're not going to keep drinking water all night, you're going to have your first gin.

James (*sharply*)   The kid's a natural non-drinker! If he's a water-baby, he's a water-baby!

Rosie, *surprised at this protective attitude.*

Oh, it's got nothing to do with me.

Edmund   I should like to attempt one gin, everyone appeared so happy at the inn. And I should not like to appear an outsider.

Edmund *raises his glass apprehensively, self-consciously. He drinks and is pleased with the experiment.*

Cheers! What convivial hosts! (*Looks towards small room.*)
But will we not awaken the children.

James (*motions him to bend closer*)   Come here, I'll tell you
about that. I would be afraid to give a woman a baby,
Edmund. Once a woman has a baby she's first-rate happy
then and man isn't so so-so-so, yeh know, anymore. (*For her
confirmation.*) Rosie?

Rosie   Man is only a tool, Edmund.

Edmund   But what is wrong with making someone
happy?

James   And what about me?

Edmund   You want to have a baby?

James   Aw Jesus! – Aw, Edmund! Don't be silly. He
doesn't understand –

Rosie   That's what I've been saying. But it's nice.

Edmund   I understand.

James   What?

Edmund   Giving happiness gives one pleasure. In youth
I was told, you can't do –

James   You can't do a good thing too often! Rosie?

James *and* **Rosie** *laugh bawdily.* **Edmund** *smiling innocently.*

(*Laughing scornfully.*) He doesn't get it! (*Continues laughing,
growing frustrated.*) He doesn't get it, he doesn't get it! – I
don't get it now! – What does it matter? – Hate smelly
babies! – Hate them!

Silence.

Rosie *offers to top up* **Edmund**'*s glass.* **Edmund** *refuses.*

(*Irritably.*) Why not?

Edmund   I recognise its merit but will remain with the twofold elevation of the one: savour and the virtue of its moderation.

James   Well, can you sing?

Edmund   I can.

James   Will you?

Edmund   I will.

James *and* **Rosie** *settle themselves anticipating something pleasant.* **Edmund** *sings the first line 'Down in the forest' and delivers the remainder in wonder.*

Down in the forest . . . I saw her. And my being fed to regeneration. And the meaning of everything became clear and unimportant. And once I closed my eyes to trap the angel self within me, but all of me had fused to become one sensitive eye, drinking in God, or was I radiating Him? or was I Him?

James   Not bad!

Rosie   Very good!

Edmund   Not finished. Then. (*He shivers.*) Down in the forest . . . I lay upon the fallen leaves, the only noise was dying hushed derision. And then the quietness of a smile, so strange and still, no sound to cheer the accomplishment of journey's end, for my mission was quite done. And then I lookéd up to see a crow alighting from a tree, to perch upon my breast. I wondered at his fearless apathetic eye more beadier than fish's fixed on mine, and I wondered at his mystery purpose: 'twas not good. The cakéd offal on his beak was grey, and then he ope'd it up to show the stiffened corpse of maggot for a tongue. I knew that birds are sometimes known in vagary to offer their own store to human kind, and so I thought I would accept, to please the crow for he was dark, his succulence, his relish, my disgust. And then I checked my mouth to find that it was shut as in paralysis. And then – O God! – my eyes I found

were open with such tautness: they were gaping bulges
wide. And though I would I could not race my fear
towards liberating climax, to release me in a roar. And on
and on the insult of my tightened lips I staréd back in the
innocence of silent nightmare. And then he pecked; I was
so young, and that was that.

Pause. **Edmund** *smiling.*

James   I was so young, I played it straight –

Rosie (*as in a panic*)   We played it straight, James, we
played it straight –

James   Who's talking?

Rosie   You are.

James   What is the past?

Rosie   A fairytale.

James   Shut up. A broken promise. Wouldn't it be better
to – I don't mean frighten the daylights out of babies – but
to warn them a bit. Yeh know. A few rotten hints now and
again and that.

Rosie   Forearmed is –

James   Shut up. You were about to say?

Edmund   Mary Rose was speaking.

Rosie   I'm finished.

James (*to her*)   What? – (*To him.*) What?

Edmund   But was not the past golden, nevertheless?

James   Yes – yes – yes, very golden nevertheless. What
came after?

Rosie   Sing us a song, James, tell us a story – Oh he has a
lovely story, personal and subjective.

James   Not personal! Only any old story! Now!

Edmund   Do narrate, but I must anon be gone to
continue my search for Anastasia.

James   For who? (*He has forgotten all about her.*)

Edmund   Anastasia.

Rosie (*answering* **James**' *puzzlement*)   Anastasia!

James (*remembers*)   Yes, well, yes.

Rosie   The story, James.

Edmund   The title.

James   No title! Once upon a time there was a boy, as
there was always and as there always will be, and he was
given a dream, his life. His mother told him do not be
naughty, who would be naughty, no one is naughty. And
there would be a lovely girl for him one day, and she
would have blue eyes and golden hair. His mother was
very very beautiful and good. His father taught him
honesty, to stand erect and be sincere and tell no lies, like
every other person in the world, his brothers. And that on
the stroke of twelve on his twenty-first birthday he would
become a man, and he would not be afraid to have his
appendix out, and he would get better and better and
better. And the teachers too were saintly men and could
answer all his questions. They told him of the good laws,
and how bad laws could not work because they were bad.
And sums, so as not to burden anybody with his ignorance
in the years ahead, his life. And the books he read were
filled with heroes; people lived happily, ugliness was sure
to turn to beauty, and poor boys were better than rich
boys because they were noble really, and they married the
loveliest girl you ever saw, and she had blue eyes and
golden hair. And the church told him of God, kind God
and guardian angels. And how everyone is made just like
God – even the little boy himself was. There was a devil
but he was not alive; he was dead really. And the kindest
stork you ever saw with a great red beak would take care
of any works and pomps. And there was a king there for –

that was not quite clear. But he was there, like in all the other stories. Not that anything would go wrong, but he was keeping an eye on things all the same. Not that anything could go wrong. He was there, probably, to make the boy's life his dream.

Edmund   Bravo! Exceeding lovely, James indeed!

James   Not finished. Yes, everyone gave the little boy balloons, the most expensive kind, already inflated, yellow, green, blue and red, the very best of colours, and they floated above him, nodding and bobbing, and lifting his feet clear off the ground so that he never had to walk a step anywhere. Until, one day, one of them burst, and it was the beautiful blue one. And he was not prepared for this. So, one day, he walked away into the forest forever.

Rosie   And one by one the other balloons burst.

Edmund   A naughty little boy.

James   What?

Edmund   For bursting his balloons.

James   Does a little boy burst his own balloons?

Edmund   If a naughty little boy he is. And then he tries to burst the balloons of good and mannered little boys.

James   What! The very clots of people who gave them to him! What sort of monk are you?

Edmund   Those clots of people got balloons too.

James   And what happened to them? Burst! By the clots of people who gave them to them! So you'd imagine someone would learn something, wouldn't you?

Rosie   I think –

James   *You* think? *You* think? –

Rosie   Yes, I think – I say they'll have to stop bursting sometime that's all!

James   No, daftie! No, madam! They'll have to stop giving them out, that's all! (*To* **Edmund**.) Yes?

Edmund   What befell the little boy in the end?

James   Died.

Edmund   Without a –

James   No balloons, died, nothing, and he lived happily ever after.

Rosie   What about a little music?

Rosie *goes to the door of the small room and finds it locked. She tugs at the handle.* **James** *is unperturbed by her action.*

This door is locked.

Edmund   Your story was well told.

James   I'm a queer shot. I'm very well educated too, but invariably I do my moronic bit when I'm annoyed. We're annoyed see, so we don't like talking nice. Rosie? (*For her confirmation.*)

Rosie (*tugging at door handle*)   You can say that for bloody sure.

James   I used to talk nice all the time. When I'm in the driver's seat I still occasionally talk nice. Also, occasionally, when I'm chatting up crumpet. (*Explaining.*) Charvers. The thicker they are, the nicer you talk. I tried a lot of women, didn't I, Rosie?

Rosie   Yep.

James   That's in case you'd think. But while you're talking nice, because they are so thick, before you know what's happening, they've got you, a nice guy, turned into a creeping Jesus, until you've got so low you're Mephistopheles. For instance, I noticed Rosie here giving you the wink.

Edmund   But –

James No – no, no need to rebut, I don't mind. I'm in the driver's seat as it happens, but you don't understand that neither. So, to come to the point I'm coming to: if one loves, one should be in love. Do you see what I mean?

Rosie If one loves one should be in love, James. Simple alive.

James No need to embellish. I'll make a statement. I am in love. Hmm? (*Sing-songing, drunkenly, childishly.*) I am in love! – I am in love! I am going to soar, to soar, to fly, on my very last try, my very last try! Caw, caw, caw! I have found my dream, I will never wake up, my dream, my dream, my future at last!

Rosie *is laughing.*

James (*now embarrassed*)   Haw-haw, dream, Edmund! Rosie, haw, love! (*Then, wary, anticipating* **Edmund**.) Yes?

Edmund You are making your last try here?

James Not necessarily in this room. I mean – What do you mean, exactly, 'here'? I promise you I didn't want to try again. Rosie?

Rosie On the contrary.

James Can't you take a simple statement? And there's been a bastard following me about and, no matter who he is, if I catch up on him, I'll – Well, he'd better watch his P's and Q's. Yes?

Edmund This last time you are trying – Mary Rose, of course?

James Mary Rose! Mary Rose! What are you looking at my eye for? I happen to be genuinely fond of old Rosie – Mary Rose. Pretty fond of her.

He gives a hug and a little kiss to **Rosie**.

So, yeh know, you have a nice bright night outside for your search.

He goes out of the cabin, leaving the door open for **Edmund**.

Edmund (*bows to* **Rosie**)   Thank you.

Rosie   He's sobered up.

Edmund   Yes.

Rosie   Another time.

Edmund   Yes.

She purses her lips for him to kiss her.

Mary Rose –

Rosie } Just my cheek then – just my cheek –
Edmund } Believe you must that fidelity's single breach –

Rosie   For God's sake, my platonic poxy cheek!

As **Edmund** *kisses her on the cheek.*

Got him! Round two.

Edmund *goes out of the cabin.*

Third and final round coming up.

Rosie *goes to bed.*

James *sees* **Edmund** *coming out of the cabin and he hides.
Then, thinking that* **Edmund** *has gone,* **James** *is racing back to
the cabin, gleefully, and has passed* **Edmund** *before he realises*
Edmund's *presence. He returns to* **Edmund** *wearily.*

James   Yeh?

Edmund   Curiously, your story reminds me of the
parting-day my brother, coincidentally a James, left home.

James   Oh yeh?

Edmund   And from unexchangéd glances it was plain,
that twixt my ma and he, all was not well.

James   Oh yeh?

Edmund   The unshed tears and unspoken words gave an aura to our home of deploration.

James   Oh yeh?

Edmund   And though both ma and da most earnestly declared that James a saint some day would be, my languishment's remained.

James   Come to the point.

Edmund   Well, it may be so that no successful saint has James become, or even lowly living cherubim, but so much more would we love him if I could bring him home.

James   To our mountains.

Edmund   And to vales.

James   Jesus kid!

Edmund   To love.

James   To dress him up in hope again?

Edmund   He need not be ashamed.

James   For a new batch of balloons for a new batch of pins?

Edmund   James –

James   Jee-sus kid! Did it not occur to you that this James character – whoever he might be – might be choking with their home-made love and mem-o-ries?

Edmund   My brother James is –

James   Did it never strike you pink that he might really be a mean-un?

Edmund   James –

James   Then you look out! Cause twill strike you blind and strike you dumb when you find out, suddenlike, he is no funny man and not a fool. That he's a volunteer for dirty deeds, that he's mightily proud of getting worse, that

he aims to hit rock-bottom, for his basis. Now, if you'll
take my advice you'll go home, and tell those bringing-in-
the-sheafers that you met the man who has escaped. He's
not their victim anymore. You tell them that.

Edmund　But, James, you have misunderstood.

James　No-no-no-no now, baby! Don't you try to
sweetheart me again. We've had that bit.

Edmund　But, James –

James　And let's have done with the innocent shit. See,
I'm a believer in honest, open ignorance, not innocence.
Don't you confuse the two like the hypocrites like to do.
They manured our honest open ignorance on moral crap
and fairy snow, then sent us out as innocents to chew the
ears off any man, wife, stranger, friend, and kick their
hearts to death in the name of Jesus Christ or Santa Claus
to boot. (*To himself.*) Till you don't know where you are or
what you are or –

Edmund ⎱ James, you are my –
James ⎰ Who are you! I don't know who I am but I'm
　　　　　not going to be no sunlamplit brother of
　　　　　anyone!

Edmund *opens his mouth to speak.*

Jesus, he will not listen to me!

Edmund *opens his mouth.*

No! Look, leave me alone, I'm tired, I've been on the go!
(*A plead.*) Rock-bottom for my basis, what's wrong with
that? I must get my feet on the ground, Edmund. My mind
is such a coloured kite, Edmund. I've got so much crap to
unload, you would not believe! It's a simple case of honest
terra firma or caput for me. Do you dig?

Edmund *nods.*

You're codding me now?

Edmund *shakes his head.*

And I'm such a weary little dear. Isn't that honest of me?

Edmund *nods*.

Well, let's split for now and hit for bunkeroonysville. Hmm?

Edmund *looks sad*.

. . . I need my kip, Edmund. (*Sighs*.)

Yeh?

Edmund   I have a message for my brother.

James   That's as maybe. Yeh?

Edmund   Granddaddy died.

James   Oh yeh?

Edmund   Grandmammy outlasted him by seven minutes.

James   Oh yeh.

Edmund   Father died.

James   Oh yeh?

Edmund   Mother is dead . . . Ma is dead.

James   Oh yeh?

Edmund   She said to tell James she forgave him. She was old and yellow and withered and grey, her hands worn with care when she died. Even the King was there, his last respects to pay. But it was you she wanted to hear say you loved her.

James   He die?

Edmund   What?

James (*harshly*)   The King – the King!

Edmund   He did.

James   Good.

Edmund   Say it to the night, James.

James (*quietly*)   You won't give up, will you?

Edmund   She will hear you.

James   That crow will come and peck the bubbles of your eyes.

Edmund   You can feel her in the night, listening, waiting.

James   Look, I'm sure you had a nice mother, kid, you know.

Edmund   You can say that sincerely, without prevarication?

James (*prevaricating*)   Ah-hmm? – Yeh.

Edmund   Perhaps I have been on another erring tack. I'll continue my search for Anastasia.

Edmund *exits.*

James *considers calling* **Edmund** *back and relinquishing* **Anastasia**. *He changes his mind. He trots into the cabin.* **Rosie** *is asleep. He gets* **Edmund**'s *sword from under the bed and deliberately nicks his finger with the point. He smears his blood on the blade. He unlocks the door of the little room and goes in to* **Anastasia**. *He holds the blood-stained sword under her nose.*

James   He's dead!

He thrusts the sword into the floor so that it stands upright.

The lights fade.

Scene Six

Moonlight. **James** *is sitting outside the cabin waiting-up for cock-crow; occasionally glances back at the cabin where he has left* **Anastasia**.

James (*trying to be poetic*)   Ah, the moon! . . . The moon, the moon, that . . . orb! That . . . Come on, old cock,

crow! A nice early crow this morning . . . That . . . orb!
Crow, just once, good cock, and I will be hers and she,
mine, our lives to begin together, forever: What a lovely
little signal she chose! . . . Crow!

He dozes, wakes with a start, flicking his hand across his forehead.

Nickerdehpazzee! Dead hand so mottled, brown so worn
with care! I'll nail you witch! I'll nail you! . . . But how?
Speak well of them that persecute you. Who said that? The
cunning of it. Some bury them with a smile and a tear,
some with a prayer and a nail . . . I'll try. (*Braces himself,
begins with an effort.*) God gave me a wonderful mammy, her
memory will never grow old, her smile was – (*Angrily.*)
Aw, yes – yes, her memory, heart, smile, head, hands,
promises! . . . What am I doing here, mooning? I swore
never more. Why, properly pruned of the dead wood I
could be almost anything . . . Who said that? . . . That
poxy-looking prick of an orb up there! Just another
American ad now! . . . (*Wearily, dozing.*) Aw, but when
that cocky chap crows, just once . . . (*Groans.*) Jimmy . . .
(*He falls asleep.*)

Morning lights the cabin.

We can now see into the cabin. The chair that **Anastasia** *was
bound to in the small room is vacant. The sword remains upright
stuck in the floor, the back of the chair up against it, and lengths of
rope are strewn on the floor. The suggestion is that* **Anastasia**
*manoeuvred the chair into this position and freed herself. There is no
sign of* **Anastasia**. *(She is hiding in the room but we do not see
her.)*

Rosie *gets out of bed, yawning, looks about for* **James**; *old
slippers, an old dressing gown. She comes out of the cabin speaking
in her morning baby voice.*

Rosie   My Jamie sity (*sitting*) upy all nighty. Why, Jame-
Jame?

James (*awakes*)   Ah?!

Rosie   Naughty, Jamie, catchy coldy.

James (*absently*)   The bastard cock, why doesn't he crow?

Rosie *laughs, not understanding, and bends to kiss him. He pushes her away.*

Rosie   Not nicey. And you behaved so well last nighty. Such a lovely timey.

James   Crow! My God, it must be nearly twelve o'clock!

Rosie   And poor Edmund searching in the forest all night. Oh, look! There's some villagers going off to help him. They all love him. Were you sity upy in sympathy with him? That's nicey. Cockadeedle-doo! There, you're free of your nicey gesture! My Jamie was such a clever, masterful Jame-Jame last night, arguing with Mund-Mund. And my Jame-Jame won.

James (*absently, referring to cock*)   What is the matter with him?

Rosie   But Mund-Mund doesn't have to talkey: he looks it.

James (*absently*)   He looks it.

Rosie   Such a lovely face. Such a sure face. I think he thinks you are his brother. Oh, I wish you were related. Then we would be nearer!

James (*thinks he hears something*)   Shh! – Shh! . . . (*Absently.*) Nearer?

Rosie   Closer.

James   Who?

Rosie   Why, the three of us.

James   For a start, pig, there's nothing between us.

Rosie   You called me wifey yesterday.

James   What does that mean, today or any day? Have we the bit of paper to prove it? Did we have the rings, the candles, the bells, the balls, the first night, the honeymoon, the blushes?

Rosie   Now, Jame-Jame, remember I wanted to –

James   Jamie, Jame-Jame! My name is James! ROSIE!

Rosie (*urgently*)   Let's not quarrel, James, we don't want to quarrel, James, we vowed, we agreed a million times we wouldn't quarrel.

James (*sneering*)   And you believed? You believed?

Rosie   Stop, James, please, I can't stand it!

James   I can! I can!

Rosie   You can't, James.

James   Rosie! Rosie!

Rosie   My name is –

James   Rosie! Rosie!

Rosie   Mary Ro –

James   Rosie! Rosie! Rosie!

Rosie   Mary! Mary! Mary!

James   Rosie, the delicate thing, female!

Rosie   Jame-Jame, sniveller, cry-in-bed dreamer!

James   The middle-aged girl!

Rosie   Thirty-seven!

James   Get your supporting harnesses on, your teeth out of the cup, princess!

Rosie   The princess that this corsetted ponce dragged into filth and scum, until she became filth and scum –

James   You said it! – You said it! –

Rosie   From *his* touch!

James   Slut, harlot!

Rosie   The senile ponce! – How's your back?

James   You excuse for a whore!

Rosie   That kept you, dog, in bread!

James   What about my kiss last night? – What about my kiss last night? –

Rosie   Look at it! – Behold it! – Man! –

James   Didn't it fool you? – Didn't it fool you? –

Rosie   Look at it? Lover!

James   Didn't it fool you for this morning?

Rosie   Didn't I fool you by calling you strong and clever for last night? –

James   Didn't I fool you? –

Rosie   When I knew you were acting, pretending, loading the argument –

James   I wasn't loading the –

Rosie   Giving him the questions for your rehearsed answers!

James   Not rehearsed! I wanted him to win!

Rosie   Didn't I fool you? – Didn't I fool you? –

James   Oh, but I forgot, Mary Rose is in love with Mund-Mund!

Rosie   Didn't I fool you when I knew you'd be chasing another rainbow today?

James   But didn't I know you didn't mean it?

Rosie   Look – look – look, out there, quick –

James   Didn't I know you didn't mean it? –

Rosie   Run and catch your rainbow, little crying cringing man!

James   But didn't I know you didn't mean it, so it doesn't affect me! –

Rosie   Didn't I know –

James   'Cause I had this quarrel planned! Now!

Rosie   Didn't I know your twisted mind would be thinking that way? –

James   And because I planned it, it hurts you more! Now!

Rosie   And because I can see through your bottle-glass head spoils that! Now!

James   But do you know the reason I didn't marry you all this time? Because now, when you look like pus and thirty-seven, I can laugh and walk away!

Rosie   But who else would have you? Didn't you try-oi?

James   And you didn't try-oi, I suppose?

Rosie   Oh, but nothing can stop me loving Edmund and comparing him with you!

James   But that's the poi-oint: nobody can stop you, *nobody* wants to!

Rosie   But, really, you do compare very well with him, James, really.

James   And you with Anastasia!

Rosie   And, really, I shall go on loving him. It's simple, really, to love him: A man. Everyone loves him. Everyone loves you, Jame-Jame?

James   . . . Rosie!

Rosie   Everyone loves you, Jame-Jame?

James   Rosie! – Rosie! – Rosie!

Rosie   Mary Rose! – Mary! – Mary! – Prick!

James   Whore, harridan, slut, shrew! –

Rosie   Pencil prick!

James   Oh yeah? – Oh yeah?

Rosie   Unforgettable pencil prick!

James   Oh yeah? – Oh – Shh!

Off, the cock crows. **James** *delighted.* **Rosie** *is suspicious but hides it.*

Rosie   I mean, he's good-looking, symmetrical, interesting, educated, elegant, speaks beautifully, assured, unwarty . . . Shall I go on? I've lots more.

James *smiles, inviting her to continue.*

I pray he finds her, just to annoy you. Did you think I didn't know you would be after her? Mooching about in the wood yesterday. James and Anastasia! Tck! Pathetic! And your poor old back! It's too laughable.

James   Finished?

Rosie   That depends, thank you.

James *trots cockily into the cabin.* **Rosie** *hurries after him.*

James   Well . . . (*Gathers his thoughts.*) You don't know what I'm going to say to you now, do you?

Rosie   Something inspiring. Maybe, 'You can't say two kind words to me'.

James   No, my dear. Perhaps you should sit down . . . As you please. But this will come as something of a little shock. Well, I visited her last night. You know, *her*, hmm? While you lay gently sleeping. *I* have got her, *I* found her, she is hidden, safe and all mine. A short visit, necessarily, just to inform her that Edmund was dead. Tripped on a tree root, impaled on his sword. Out of propriety, we agreed that there should be a short period of mourning; a period which might be spent profitably in considering the undesirability of force. And so, we promised to be ready for each other at cock-crow. You're silent, my dear? But then you are thinking this is the pay off and you are right, so it is. But let us not be pecuniary in parting.

Rosie   Acrimonious.

James   . . . As you will, my dear, I meant exactly what I said, but as you will if it gives you solace. Rosie, you are through. But let us not be pecuniary or acrimonious in parting. I have grounds on which to be grateful to you, and I hereby acknowledge the amount of my debt. *You* were the grounds on which I made my first and last mistakes. And yours was the oppression of some nineteen years' duration that encouraged my imagination to evolve principles on which I should conduct my life, given a second chance.

Rosie   Am I expected to praise you?

James   Well, perhaps you will show a more appreciative reaction to the unerring fashion in which I have developed matters when I tell you where my flower awaits me.

It strikes **Rosie** *suddenly that* **Anastasia** *is hidden in the small room: her head swings about to look in that direction.* **James**, *triumphant, trots to the door of the small room.*

Clever? Come now, you will admit the obviousness of the hiding place is its inspiration. Come, magnanimity! It passed the twenty-four hour test of your pocket-searching mind. No?

Rosie   James, you're a loser.

James   Think so?

Rosie   I know so. I've lived too long with you, and you talk too much about success.

James   Think so?

Rosie   Edmund will be back.

James   Too late! Should Edmund return, she will have taken the tragic step, voluntarily. He will be undone.

Rosie   He won't, you know. He'll always be that comic step ahead of you.

James (*laughs confidently*)   Through your prayers, no doubt. (*Unlocking the door of small room.*) Pack your bag, my dear.

Rosie (*losing her composure*)   Close your eyes every time she spits!

James   As you say, my dear.

Rosie   You can't win!

James   We'll see. Be gone when I come out. And so, farewell.

James *goes into the small room. His consternation on finding the vacant chair, looking incredulously at a piece of severed rope, a window which is firmly closed. He is searching on his hands and knees when* **Anastasia** *emerges from behind the door, gets the sword and has it held aloft to smite him when* **Rosie** *gives the warning cry.*

Rosie   James!

The cry gives halt to **Anastasia**'*s stroke. She drops the sword, which* **James** *catches, and runs out of the cabin.* **James** *is transfixed with shock. When he rises he moves about erratically, beating himself to allay his terror and frustration.*

Rosie *is laughing – continues laughing to end of scene.*

Anastasia'*s escape is confused and she circles the cabin a few times, her movement distracted.*

The lights are fading. **James** *is coming out of the cabin to give chase, carrying the sword.*

Scene Seven

Another part of the forest.

Anastasia *is sitting on a height that overlooks a ravine, singing her suicide song.*

Through the song **James** *enters stealthily (on the ground level below her).*

Anastasia.

> I'm young but not too young to know
> I've met the one I loved to love,
> The one who wandered in my soul,
> So tall and fine.
> From early days my dreams did tell
> His path and mine converging,
> The cross-roads would be waiting,
> As sure as sure can be.
> And then he came and found me,
> And I could have wept for mirth,
> And the angels answered with a song:
> Immaculate! Immaculate!
> But now he's gone, no song is left,
> Life is no more, I welcome death,
> In yon ravine I go to join
> My lost love so noble and fine.

She is about to throw herself into the ravine, **James** *opens his mouth to call 'No' when:*

Edmund (*off*)   Anastasiaaaa!

Edmund *sweeps in — or comes in swinging through the trees.*
James *in a frenzy of impotent gestures.* **Edmund** *and*
Anastasia *embrace, stand apart, embrace and apart again. Their two minds become one, excitedly gushing the following*:

But, Anastasia!

Anastasia   Oh, my Edmund!

Edmund   Anastasia! —

Anastasia   Edmund! – Edmund!

Edmund   But I knew I would find you!

Anastasia   I knew it too!

Edmund   How lost was my feeling! –

Anastasia   But I would have died! –

Edmund   Bursting the sky! –

Anastasia   Without you –

Edmund   Anastasia –

Anastasia   Without you!

Edmund   Then I heard your voice –

Anastasia   I did not know I sang –

Edmund   From another world to guide me –

Anastasia   Cause our spirits were not lost –

Edmund   But mingled in the ether –

Anastasia   Searching for the anchor –

Edmund   Of each other –

Anastasia   And you came! –

Edmund   We are found!

Anastasia   Forever! –

Edmund   Together! –

Anastasia   Till death! –

Edmund   And after! –

Anastasia   And even the past –

Edmund   Was ours –

Anastasia   Yes! –

Edmund   Yes-yes! –

Anastasia   All time –

Edmund   Was made –

Anastasia   For sober –

Edmund   Sublime –

Anastasia   Glorious –

Edmund   Us! –

Anastasia   Us – us – weee! –

Edmund } The two of us!
Anastasia } The two of us!

They laugh.

James, *a small figure below them, is now watching them in wonder.*

Edmund   How much do I love you?

Anastasia   Mars, the stars! –

Edmund   Nine hundred and eighty! –

Anastasia   Three million, ten million! –

Edmund   Seventy-seven, billion trillion! –

Anastasia   Sufficiently –

Edmund   Completely –

Anastasia   So much –

Edmund   I am not me –

Anastasia   More than I can –

Edmund   Because of you –

Anastasia   I am something great –

Edmund   The trees in the streams –

Anastasia   I want to laugh or to cry –

Edmund   Both are the same –

Anastasia   For being, for looking at you –

Edmund   My lovely Anastasia –

Anastasia   Edmund, Oh my Edmund –

Edmund   Will you be my wife?

Anastasia   Yes.

They kiss.

James, *childlike, claps his hands once, silently, and stands for a moment wondering what to do. Then he hurries off excitedly.*

Scene Eight

Another part of the forest.

Rosie *enters, carrying suitcase, as if leaving* **James**. *But she is looking behind her, hoping* **James** *is following her. No sign of* **James**. *She sits on a log, sighs, smoking a cigarette.*

Then, **James**' *voice, gallantly, off.*

James (*off*)   Rosieeeee!

A moment later, **James** *enters at a run, poses gallantly, sword held high.* **Rosie** *exhaling smoke apathetically.*

Rosie (*cynically*)   Did you kill her?

James   Ah . . . No.

Rosie *turns away.* **James** *trying to maintain his gallant effort against her apathy and, indeed, her appearance. His next call startles her a little.*

Rosieeeee! I mean, Rosie . . . I'm very sorry about this morning. All our marital altercations. They shall never happen again. Forgive me, now, yeh know.

Rosie   I'm used to it.

James   Ah, the cigarette. Could you . . . ?

Rosie   What?

James   I mean –

Rosie   Have you none, are you out, James?

James   No – no, I'll have a puff.

He takes the cigarette, has a drag of it to hide the fact that he merely wants to get rid of it. He stubs it out. **Rosie** *is puzzled.*

Rosie   I'm sorry too. What? And for laughing at you. Hmmm?

James   Your hair.

Rosie   It's awful.

James   No, it's . . . not awful. (*He poses again, putting his foot on the log.*) Magic – Magic mirror on the wall, who is the fairest one of all? Rosie is!

Rosie (*pleased*)   Oh, James, what's wrong with you? (*Her hand stealing towards his crotch.*)

James   No, no, but I mean to say, like, if you look at it this way, we waste an awful lot of time, Mary Rose, flower, and I could take you a million places. Three million!

Rosie   But the money –

James   No, don't mind that for now. Well, many places.

Rosie } We could row.
James } We could go to – What?

Rosie   Row.

James   Yes. We could . . . row.

Rosie   Where to?

James   Japan. To Europe.

Rosie   Together?

James   To the moon.

She laughs, pleased.

. . . We'll drink in life —

Rosie   The Garden of Eden —

James   Heaven —

Rosie   And hell — just to see what it's like.

James   And I'll protect you.

Rosie   And love me —

James   And love me —

Rosie   And *me*, James —

James   Yes!

Rosie   Unceasing —

James   *That*'s it!

Rosie   Till death us do part —

James   And it never will, Rosie, Mary Rose, Mary!

Rosie   Oh, Jimmy, we'll kiss our way to paradise —

James   And the thrill of your kiss will constantly fire me to great things.

Rosie   The thrill of a kiss!

They look at each other. They kiss nervously, shyly. Immediately there is a collapse.

(*Forcing a laugh.*) That was a laugh, James . . . We could try again. My fault. I didn't understand. I'll take one of my slimming pills.

James   Don't bother.

Rosie   What?

James   They might help. (*He sighs*.)

Rosie   They've got things in them.

James (*harshly*)   Naaw! Don't!

Rosie (*tearfully*)   Love you, James.

James   Nonsense, bollocks, nonsense! Oh, Jesus!

Rosie   Little Jesus!

James   I just want to stop!

Rosie   Little Jesus!

James   I was only trying for something, for anything.

Rosie   For both of us.

Pause.

James   I really do try, don't I? Tell me. I tried a lot of things, didn't I?

Rosie   Yes.

James   I mean, despite appearances, I've been on the go. So, it's not my fault, is it?

Rosie   We don't understand.

James   Who understands.

Rosie   Nobody.

James   And don't let them tell you otherwise.

Rosie   . . . Don't let them tell me what?

James (*can't remember*)   . . . That's more of it!

Rosie   . . . We're two of a kind, James.

James (*non-committal*)   Mmm.

Rosie   Birds of a feather . . . Flocked together.

James   And the cow jumped over the moon.

Rosie *laughs.*

And who'd blame him? . . . (*Then, sudden vehemence.*) I'll tell him a thing or two.

Rosie   And her!

James   Why shouldn't I?

Rosie   Why not?

James   I could mess him up.

Rosie   Give him some facts.

James   Then see his sunny world.

He takes up the sword and shows her the hilt.

Look at that! Just look at that!

Rosie   A crest.

James   The King's crest. That was a present from the King.

Rosie (*produces* **Edmund**'s *water-flask*)   And I nicked his water-flask. Oh look! It's (*the crest*) on this too.

James   They'd fetch a pretty penny.

Rosie   Stick to the point, James, give him some facts.

James   When he comes back for those things –

Rosie   Yes!

James   I'll tell him about smells – worse –

Rosie   Unmentionables! –

James   Mention them!

Rosie   The rotten teeth! –

James   The nagging! –

Rosie   Spectacles!

James   What?

Rosie   Other pathetic things! People talking!

James   Peeping-toms.

Rosie   If they have one kid, why haven't they two.

James   Or three –

Rosie   Why haven't they four −

James   Or twelve −

Rosie   Rabbits!

James   Or none.

Rosie   Or none.

They look at each other. They continue sadly.

James   If we had a little girl, what would we tell her?

Rosie   And she'd only turn out like me . . . And a boy.

James   A son . . .

Rosie   Like you.

James   Yes.

Pause.

Rosie   Like scattered toys unable to play with each other, they say.

James.

> God gave me a wonderful mammy,
> Her memory will never grow old,
> Her smile was fashioned of sunshine,
> Her heart was purer than gold.

Rosie (*absently*)   Once, in the dark, with a client, in that boxy room, in the silence, for a moment, a child cried from the heights of the floor above.

James.

> It broke my heart to lose you,
> But you did not go alone,
> Part of Jimmy went with you
> The day you were taken home.

Rosie   And from the depths of the floor below, from the basement, for a moment, the shuffling of that blind old man stopped.

James   Loving memory.

Rosie   Scattered toys.

Pause.

James   You know, Rose, if he ever knew – really knew – the way we are, the way we live.

Rosie   Oh, if she knew, if she ever knew, James.

James   Up on his high rocking-horse of morality . . . (*Vehemently.*) Think! What else can we tell them? But there are hundreds of horrible things! . . . Are you thinking?

Rosie   I am, James.

James   . . . But there are millions of rotten things!

Rosie   Well . . .

James   What?

Rosie   Well, about men.

James   What about men?

Rosie   Well, how they're not so much men.

James   Don't be afraid, this is too important.

Rosie   I mean how he'll more likely be afraid of mice than she will.

James   And how she'll more likely have to provide the bread!

Rosie   And how men get tired of one bed!

James   And women too – more often –

Rosie   I agree, I agree. And how hard it is to find friends –

James   That aren't enemies.

Rosie   And not be their enemies for being friends.

James   Yes – yes!

Rosie   And about getting old!

James   Yes! Get them with the obvious!

Rosie   I'm doing alright, James, amn't I? –

James   The surprise of the obvious.

Rosie   But you do like me, James, don't you? –

James   And success! 'Cause there's no such thing. –
That's right – And how it looks bad, if they're nice or not
nice to each other in public.

Rosie   Yes. (*Apathetically.*) –

James   And how they'll run out of conversation, hmm?

Rosie   That's a good one –

James   And . . . No, it would be no use.

Rosie   How?

James   You can never tell his kind anything.

Pause.

They continue, mellow.

Rosie   But I must tell you, I'm pretty taken by him.

James   Pretty taken . . . I was watching them in the
wood.

Rosie   I'm sure it was grand.

James   Pretty taken . . . He's a prince, yeh know.

Rosie   What? – Edmund? – A real one? – Really?

James   Yeh.

Rosie   Well-well!

James   He's my brother.

Rosie   What? . . . Aw, come off it! You're a prince too?

James   No. No, I'm not. I'm not a prince. Yeh see, he's a
half-brother, like.

Rosie   Seriously?

James   Serious.

Rosie   But how?

James   Well . . . a certain king who ruled at home come our ways one day to shelter in the barn out of the rain. And my mother, well, in the barn, they – she – well, Edmund's the King's son. The King even visited her before she died. Crest on sword, the (*water-flask*.) . . .

Rosie   Well, I never! . . . So Edmund's a prince and you're not.

James   That's about it.

Rosie   That's not fair, James.

James   That's life. (*He sighs*.) . . . Oh, I wasn't a peeping-tom at the time: it was natural, yeh know, for me to be in the barn. Well, I was a pious little lad and I'd decided for myself to work hard around the stables and that, to help my parents out, so that if a baby brother came along, he would be given the chances, the money would be there for his education. Yeh know. Maybe I should have overlooked it, him being a king and all. But the tremors of that stormy day soon revealed other cracks in the walls, hitherto institutions with unblemished surfaces.

Rosie (*suddenly*)   Did he have his crown on?

James   Aw, it's too depressing.

Rosie   Poor love.

James   I suppose you must know now, Rose, that I'm not at all well-educated. Sweeping out the stables. I've always lied about my education.

Rosie   It doesn't matter.

James   It does, it does. When I gam on (*pretend*) educated, I'm aping you.

Rosie   We're very similar people, James.

James   We are. And a confession: I'm always thinking I'm better. But we are. Even a few minutes ago when you said, we're two of a kind –

Rosie   Birds of a feather –

James   I didn't want to agree.

Rosie   I understand, James.

James   But we are.

Rosie   We have an awful lot in common.

Short pause.

James   Do you remember, Rose – Wait a minute. Were we? . . . Yes! When we were in love. Do you?

Rosie   . . . We wouldn't –

James ⎫   We wouldn't go to bed at night!
Rosie ⎭   We wouldn't go to bed at night!

James   Trying to stay awake!

Rosie   In case we'd miss a single second of it all.

James   I wanted to be you.

Rosie   I wanted to be you!

James   I wanted to be you!

Rosie   You wrote me poems, James.

James   I thought – Don't laugh – I used to imagine if only the two of us could breathe from the same lungs.

Rosie   Beautiful . . . What happened to it?

James   (*gesturing as if pricking a balloon with a pin*)   Puck! Sssssssss!

Pause.

Rosie   I thought we might stop all this kind of thing here
. . . And you were planning to leave me.

James   How do you know that?

Rosie   Instinct. A woman's. And you often thought of it
before . . . What do you think?

James   What?

Rosie   About leaving me.

James   Did you ever think about leaving me?

Rosie   I did, but I wouldn't.

James   You're nicer than me, Rosie.

Rosie   I am not, James, I know it.

James   No. I know better. I'm rotten. And I'm afraid of
what I'm going to be like in ten years' time.

Pause.

Rosie   We aren't succeeding with anything here.

James   I don't know.

Rosie (*absently*)   Hmm?

James   I don't know, Rose. 'God gave me a wonderful
mammy': I said that easily enough.

Rosie   Hmm?

James   I shed that easily enough.

Rosie   (*like a first realisation*)   But we're very good
friends, James.

James (*absently*)   What?

Rosie   We're very good friends.

James (*coming alive*)   What? Aren't we? We are! . . . And
do you know it's as good as – it's better than – What? – it's
much better than love!

Rosie   Yes, but we can still love, now and again.

James (*not listening*)   Yes, we can, but we're very good friends, we are very good friends.

The excitement of the feeling makes him trot about.

Rosie   Where are you going?

James   No, I wasn't going anywhere. Have to move.

He stops, looks at her.

I enjoyed that little chat.

They smile at each other, then look away shyly.
They look at each other again and start to laugh, enjoying the warmth of the moment.
They laugh so long it tends towards hysteria.

Rosie   Dear, oh dear! . . .

James   Maybe we'll be crying in a minute . . .

Rosie   What harm. I feel so good.

James   Oh, don't trust it, Rosie!

Rosie   . . . Taunting us again . . .

James   . . . I just got an idea! . . .

Rosie   Let's not scheme, James . . .

James   Oh, it would keep us laughing for a while . . . If we were in bad humour we'd use it.

The laughter grows weaker, sporadic. **James** *stops;* **Rosie** *stops a little later.*

Rosie   What were we laughing at?

James   . . . That's more of it!

Rosie   I felt so grateful. (*A titter escapes.*)

James   Why should he have it all when the world treats us this way?

Rosie   So indiscriminately.

James (*sharply*)   I know – I know! Why don't I just go along and acknowledge him as my brother?

Rosie   That's because – (*Another titter escapes.*) because you're ashamed of yourself.

James   Oh! Is it? You understand it all, do you, with your guilt-ridden little Jesus education!

Pause.

Rosie *smiles evilly a moment before* **James** *speaks.*

If they were like us . . .

Rosie *nods, continues smiling.*

What?

Rosie   Yesss.

James   If we can't get to their ridiculous level, they must be brought to ours.

Rosie   I'm way ahead of you. I've most of the spade-work done.

James (*he grins appreciatively*)   A taste for gin.

Rosie   He has kissed my hand, my cheek . . .

James   . . . When he comes back for those things – (*The sword, the flask.*)

Rosie   A pleasure, James. Round three coming up.

James   And, meanwhile, I'll look after the orphan. Let's get a few details worked out.

They hurry off.

Scene Nine

Night. The cabin. The cabin appears transformed. (Softly lit; an arrangement of flowers; soft music.) **Rosie** *and* **Edmund** *have dined.* **Rosie** *wears a sexy dress.* **Edmund** *appears quite drunk.*

Outside, **James** *is hovering impatiently, eavesdropping, waiting to hear where* **Edmund** *has left* **Anastasia**.

Rosie   More gin?

Edmund (*laughs*)   'Tis nice stuff!

Rosie (*filling* **Edmund**'*s glass*)   Isn't it? There were seven in all in my home town, once upon a time, wanted to marry me. Marriage, oh yes, no lie, Edmund, seven. As honest as their ungroping hands. They liked me for myself, you see. But I was looking for one and lost myself. Forever. Hmmm?

Edmund (*laughs*)   A feast!

Rosie   Once I knew two complete recipe books by heart. My hometown! (*She takes up the gin bottle, brushing away a tear. She finds the gin bottle empty.*) I loved my daddy. He reminded me of God, and Uncle Joe.

Edmund (*laughs*)   'Twas a feast.

Rosie   Well, not bad for one little gas ring. But let me get some more gin.

Rosie *goes into the small room for another bottle of gin.*

James *races around the cabin and speaks to her angrily through the window of the small room.*

James   What's all the sham-talk for? Get the poxy score and ascertain where he's left the orphan?

Edmund (*calls*)   But 'tis pity James could not be here!

Rosie   'Tis a pity, 'tis. But he must be a hundred and fifty miles away by now. (*Returning to* **Edmund**.) And he won't be back 'til morning.

James *to front of house to eavesdrop the better.*

Rosie *fills glasses.*

Edmund   Sad. A good fellow is James. I had wanted to bid him farewell.

Rosie   We were wondering if you found your brother.

Edmund   Now that, Mary Rose, is strange. My body is not satisfied –

Rosie   Yes, Edmund?

Edmund   Yet spirit says my quest is done.

Rosie   How strange!

Edmund   Is it not 'ceeding strange?

Rosie   How very strange! And the villain?

Edmund   The villain, ah, the bane! I started here in search of . . . ah . . . ah . . .

Rosie   Three.

Edmund   Three. I have found one.

Rosie   Yes, I wanted to ask you, how is dear Anastasia? Where have you left her?

Edmund   Found one. Found one.

Rosie   Where have you left her, Edmund?

Edmund   How kind you are to enquire and let me speak of the little one I found! How you would love her!

Rosie   But where have you left her?

Edmund   Aaa, if only she were here! But such is the rule of wedding's eve, that we one night must separate, and wear divorced affiancedment in vidual weeds to give point to spouselessness!

Rosie   Oh, and to give pause, Edmund, to heady rush towards imminent connubiality!

Edmund   Aa, quaint conservative pain, sweet I salute
your mandate celibate! But to reflect my course – to pause?
– I say go bid Niagara halt!

Rosie   Fine, okay, but where have you left her?

Edmund   But she is left in honest hands, in the house of
friendly rustics, westward on the hill.

James *races off.*

Rosie   That's all we – I wanted to know. That she is safe.

Edmund   Safe? Yes! For as I strode away, from foot of
slope I lookéd back to see my trusty friends in human
chain well-police that hut. All armed with heavy
bludgeons held aloft were they, no heathen phallic signs
they meant, but to assure this humble groom, the chaste
strength of Anastasia's belt!

Rosie *to the window to warn* **James**, *but* **James** *is gone, and
she can only shrug. Then she has perhaps a premonition about the
outcome of her own course, but she shrugs this off too and turns up the
music.*

And yet, aa, if only she were here!

Rosie   Yes, well, we're glad she's safe, but that's all I
want to hear about her. And now you must listen to the
music.

She leads him to the bed. They sit.

Edmund   How kind you are to enquire and allow me
speak of my loved one!

Rosie   } Yes, but the music –
Edmund } *(moves away from bed)*   And from afar I lookéd
                 back again to see the sun had chose this night,
                 that very hill where my love lies, to rest its
                 rubic head!

Rosie   But listen to me now, Mary Rose –

Edmund   And, Mary Rose, tomorrow's geography will place her home upon a spot, within a vale, wherein the sun doth rise.

Rosie   The sun follows her – smell them flowers.

Edmund   The sun follows her!

Rosie (*gives him the flowers*)   What fragrance! I say! A token to you, Edmund.

Edmund   I have known a flower to shed more sweet a –

Rosie   But you'll agree they smell nice? – You'll agree to that for a start.

Edmund   But yes! A toast in scent!

Rosie   A toast in scent!

Edmund   To think that eager nature should be first in her well-wishes for the morrow!

Rosie   The music, Edmund! – That's for tonight.

Edmund   Sweet, unreal, of fairies.

Rosie (*drops the stole off her shoulders*)   Soft.

Edmund   Only once before have I heard softer. A song in the forest, so pure it was a pain –

Rosie   More wine, Edmund, the mead. (*She fills his glass several times during the following.*)

Edmund (*accepts*)   'Tis nice stuff! Easing my anxious vigil for the morn that will bring my first dawn; a solace to this alone spirit that endeavours to push on the night to those first modest blushing streaks, the keys to my unity with dawn herself!

Rosie   Oh, Edmund.

Edmund   And yet, that is not all true. Yes, you are right, Mary Rose. This gin that quickens my tongue, has not so much solaced my yearnings as enhanced them. Making me

almost want these clouded hours to delay in sweetest –
sweetest taunting-hauntingness!

Rosie   Then let us lie on the bed, your hand in mine.

Edmund (*not listening*)   And with sense acute to slothful
moments now –

Rosie } Edmund –
Edmund } Know that the hours – Nay, the years, the
centuries! – following my morning union will
be the more appreciate!

Rosie (*taking his hand*)   Edmund –

Edmund (*leads her to the window*)   Come! You will watch
the heavens with me! See the clouds sweeping a path for
the feet of dawn! I have found her! (*Shouts.*) I have found
her! Have I told you? Today, Rosie!

Rosie (*alarmed, confused*)   Mary Rose, Mary!

Edmund   Down in the forest there was no crow, Rosie –

Rosie   Mary Rose, Mary!

Edmund   And my body fed, even to the skin, with a
fullness as I looked at her!

Rosie (*laughing harshly*)   Brains danced on like grapes to
make abortions!

Edmund   And once I closed my eyes to trap the angel
self within me, but no feature was left me! All of me had
fused to become one sensitive eye!

Rosie (*laughing harshly*)   I say my head is sore!

Edmund   And you too, Mary Rose, must have felt all
this.

Rosie   Rosie, Rosie, my ageing fancy grows more
incapable!

Edmund   What can I give to you, splendid earth, for all
you are giving me!

Rosie   Come to my working blanket, kiddo!

Edmund (*approaching her*)   And in what way can I thank you?

Rosie   I'm still alive, kid!

Edmund   Your garb is so thin.

Rosie   The fire of your presence is warmth for any maiden! See? Not bad? Think of the here and now. (*Dancing.*) See: Am I not alive? – See, simple alive.

Edmund   You are all that, and more.

Rosie   Then just a few of your gifts, baby!

He dances with her for a moment, then stops.

Just a dance! Just a dance!

Edmund   Understand you must that fidelity's single breach –

Rosie   All is a song, nothing is wrong for a hero, baby, they say!

He laughs, he starts to dance.

Edmund   The flowers increase their presents.

Rosie   Inhale them, inhale!

Edmund   The violins are careering towards crescendo!

Rosie   Climb with them to the heights for the cascade, baby!

Edmund   Anastasia – Anastasia!

Rosie   (*harshly, to drown him*)   Come, follow, for the crusade, baby! (*She climbs on to the bed carrying the gin bottle.*)

Edmund   Anastasia, Anastasia! (*Dances to the elevated level of small room.*)

Rosie (*sinking on to bed*)   Exhale from every pore the sweat for our cohesion! Fuse the ache, confuse the pain into joy!

Lips around my heart, strengthen me with passion! Come,
follow, hide in my wounds, in font of love, and impaled on
life, bleeding, struggling, pulsating, driving, bolting,
throbbing, spurting, scorching, crushing, holy, cannon,
war! Crusade-cascade-cascade-cascade! Edmund – James,
Jesus – Daddy, Little Jesus – Oh my baby – Us all
together! (*Joyfully*.) Everyone is fucking great, every one is
smashing! . . . Everyone . . . sinking . . . Cascade! (*She
giggles*.) . . . slowly, down . . . into the feather meadow . . .
(*Sleepily*.) and wait so peaceful for us all together, soon
again, the ferris wheel, toboggan and cascade. Hush,
drowse, Mary Rose. Little Jesus, meek and mild, thank
you for life and sleep.

Edmund   Rosie!

Short pause. **Rosie** sits up, suddenly.

Rosie (*whispers*)   Don't.

Edmund   Whore!

Rosie (*whispers*)   Don't!

Edmund   Why this betrayal?

Rosie   I thought I had a plan –

Edmund   Wherefore this attempt to sap my
foundations? –

Rosie   I thought I had a purpose –

Edmund   Whence this evil? –

Rosie   But my heart is shrivelling, tightening, getting
small, something has to happen or it will tighten into
nothing!

Edmund   Your heart is in your belly.

Rosie   Once I was a nightly abstainer, a daily
communicant!

Edmund   Wretch!

Rosie   Daddy was a Judge, Uncle Joe a Bishop!

Edmund   Jade!

Rosie   Seven in all in my home town wanted to marry me!

Edmund   Fetor! (*He is strapping on his sword and water-flask, preparing to go.*)

Rosie   No – Don't go! – I'll tell you things. James and I are not married – I've been on the game, in and out of the club. Don't go – I'll tell you things. James is your brother.

Edmund   Stop, vileness! And I suspect this serpent man of yours had a fang in this night's doings. I have a mind to wait and let the venom from his veins, but I'll bear this devil's pad no more; but will await my dawn alone, out in the dew where I'm afforded a view without stench, and with nothing to fear but the sweetness of nature.

He goes out of the cabin. The first streak of dawn appears in the sky. He exits smiling.

After a few moments **James** *enters, limping, looking beaten-up, goes into the cabin and sits.*

Rosie *is sitting on the bed, a painted-up whore. Both of them silent, dejected.*

Scene Ten

The part of the forest as in Scene One.

James *enters using a walking-stick, limping.* **Rosie** *carrying her suitcase, a moment later. He taps the ground with his stick, indicating that they will wait here.*

Rosie   Maybe they've gone off already.

James   No. They will have been getting married. Jingle bells, yeh know, and those dirty hayseed natives giving ignorant cheers.

Rosie   They might have.

James   Gone away? And left us here so happily on our own? . . . Gone off where?

Rosie   I don't know.

James   Then what are you talking about?

Rosie (*malice; watching him limping*)   . . . And are your ribs still sore?

James   Are you sure you didn't know what I was letting myself in for last night?

Rosie   No, I swear, James, honest.

James   And when you said I was his brother, he said?

Rosie   'Stop, vileness.'

James (*muttering*)   Stop, vileness.

Rosie (*to herself*)   And I felt I had him on the point of it!

James   When you said I was his brother, he said?

Rosie   I didn't want to tell him, James, but –

James   He said! – He said!

Rosie   'Stop, vileness.'

James   Well, that's alright then, isn't it? 'Stop vileness.' That's fair enough, isn't it? That's what we wanted, isn't it? Well, I shall have only one final word to say to him, one little wedding gift.

We see that the walking stick is a sword stick.

Yeh know. Now.

Rosie *does not look too happy.*

What?

Rosie   But what if *you* get killed, James?

James   So what? (*Then unconvincingly.*) So bloody what, Madam? No confidence in me, never had, always held me back.

Rosie   It's a big step.

James   You won't even encourage me to try? 'Stop, vileness' and you're not offended? You agreed with me at the start that I should wait here and have it out.

Rosie   I know I did, but . . .

James   What?

Rosie   It's a big step.

James   I know it's a big step!

Rosie (*quietly*)   And what then?

James   . . . We'll see! (*Angry.*) Well, give me an honest-to-God butchering murderer to deal with then. He'll do his job smartly. He won't ask you to kill yourself, will he? chasing a picture that isn't there, while he smiles on his approval, until, in the end, you stop, drop dead, no heart left, death-rattling, lights out, no picture! What? You prefer it this way! . . . I'm doing this for you too. I'm thinking of you too, Rose. I've been from pillar to post, pub to pub; I've abused you, Rose, and neglected you; I've been thro' thrice nine lands chasing cloud number seven, sixteen, a hundred and two, any old cloud they cared to lie on, and I've come back to you a bigger bastard every time, with the pox and my guilt! Are – you – not – offended?

Rosie (*quietly*)   And her. You're right, James.

James   Of course I'm right.

Rosie   Kill them. The two of them. But be especially cruel to her. Let them see each other age with pain, before you give the dying kick, (*Harshly.*) baby. Make them writhe, toss, implore for an end, like when sleep won't come a second night. Baby. I want to see her eyes afraid to move in snuff-dry sockets, and know that acid streams of jealousies are slowly burning channels through her head. Give them the pains of the lack of pains of motherhood. The pain of the secret birthmark, unwanted hair, wanted hair. The sanctity pain of puritan plain-Janes, and all the skin pains, from black to anaemic, until their pores are gaping holes. The pain of revenge. And the breath of fresh air, once, somewhere, and the pain that follows it because of it, breathing the stale, coffin-smelling, stifling, suffocating air of the mind. Nothing achieved but memories – that pain. Not being able – Don't let them be able – kill them, kill them, kill them.

James   I will, Rosie, I will.

Rosie   Are you sure?

James   Of course I'm sure. We have all that evil and the devil behind us.

Rosie   No devil, no evil, no God, no crap. We've tried all that. Kill them in our own name.

James   I like it, I like it!

Rosie   Let it be a fact.

James   Let it be a fact, a basis.

Rosie   Then we'll see.

James   First, I'll have him begging relationship off me, then I'll –

Rosie   Save it, James. Let us not dissipate our intention. Rather, let us fortify ourselves with a festering silence.

James   . . . Shh!

Edmund and **Anastasia** *enter, a beautiful couple, coming through the trees.*

Rosie   Shout at them.

James (*running to intercept them*)   Stop, vileness! Stop, vileness! Stop!

Anastasia   Oh, the villain, Edmund, the bane!

Edmund   Fairest of all, I commend my heart to you for the brief space of one minute.

James (*in fighting pose*)   I'm ready.

Anastasia   Oh adult Edmund bold, a favour –

James   No favours –

Anastasia   Do not dampen this our wedding day with blood.

Edmund   Granted.

James   No, I'm ready now!

Anastasia   Smile on them instead, and may happen some good will come of it.

Edmund   For in death they will rot and give out only worse stench.

Rosie   Start insulting them.

James (*to* **Rosie**)   Dignity.

Anastasia   James, though a villain, has a point left.

Rosie   May your smugness turn black, your virginity become as barren as a barrel, your –

James   Dignity, bitch! I must stay cool for this one.

Edmund   And Rosie, though unmentionably employed, may not be the worst in the world.

James   She is the worst in the world and I'm the worst in the world!

Anastasia   We have forgiven you both.

Rosie   Don't let them forgive us.

Edmund   My young wife's pleasure.

Edmund and **Anastasia** *moving away*.

Rosie   Don't let them get away.

James (*running, intercepting them*)   Stop, vileness! If I remember correct, you started here in search of your brother.

Rosie   In search of three, James.

James   Quiet, madam, don't spoil my flow!

Anastasia   He has found me.

Edmund   I have found the villain.

James   But being noble, like, you can forget your original purpose over this little scrubber.

Rosie   She would have prostrated herself for the first long-haired prick that came along wearing feathers.

Edmund (*hand on sword*)   The lowlies, true to form, in bravery assail the character of the bride.

Anastasia   Forbear, husband, we shall find you a nice brother on the way home.

James   You have found your *nice* brother.

Edmund   I give you warning!

James (*to* **Rosie**)   He won't admit it.

Rosie   'My body is not satisfied, yet spirit says, my quest is done.' Strange, is it not?

Edmund   Mark their ugliness.

Anastasia   How much lovelier we look by comparison.

James (*giggling*)   Aa, he's getting rattled.

James *and* **Edmund** *circling each other.*

Edmund   You are taking advantage of my bloodless pledge.

James   I couldn't care less about your pledge.

Edmund   Prove your claim, prove it!

James   It's a fact, it needs no proof.

Edmund   Oh, the strange fact is that one who has agreed to unrelation all along is now so eager for connection.

James (*to himself*)   Quick: what does that mean? (*To* **Edmund**.) I'm not eager to be anything to you.

Rosie   On the contrary.

James   On the contrary, I'm not eager to be anything to you.

Edmund   Then wherefore bring the subject up?

James (*growing confused*)   Then wherefore bring the . . . I-am-your-brother! You-are-going-to-admit-that. Then-I'm-going-to-have-done-with-you and deal-with-you-absolutely!

Edmund   Ridiculous.

James (*confused*)   What? (*His statement dismissed so easily.*)

Anastasia   Ridiculous.

James   Be quiet, you orphan! I can give you proof!

Rosie   He can give you proof.

James   I can give you –

Rosie   Names, addresses –

James   Who's who and what's what –

Rosie   Apple trees –

James   And meadows, now, yeh know!

Edmund   All this news I told to you myself.

Anastasia   The night they pulled you down to ginny pub-crawl.

James   There was a kind old midwife . . . what was her name . . .

Edmund   Yes, what was her name?

James   . . . There was a lame but kindly sweet-shop man . . .

Edmund (*to* **Anastasia**)   Our town is famous for non-limping men.

James   Before your time! – Before you were born!

Rosie   Get on to the spotty details of your genealogy.

James   And Teddy Bear had lost an eye and not an ear!

Edmund   Oh no!

James   Oh yes! Teddy Bear had lost an eye and lived up in the attic.

Edmund   Aha! (*Got you.*)

James   What?

Edmund   Under the stairs. Teddy Bear lived under the stairs! (*To* **Anastasia**.) I mentioned the attic to trap him.

James (*to himself*)   In the closet under the stairs, in the closet under the stairs.

Rosie   Your mother, James, before he tells us.

Edmund   I have told you all about my mother.

James   And *my* mother too. My dear old sweet mammy. God gave me a wonderful mammy, her memory will never – No, naaw, no! I've settled that score.

Edmund   And that is that! The imposter has exposed himself. I must confess I was unsure, but my final doubt he has dispelled just now. My brother James, though beautiful, could not at all speak well of ma: This flaw he had – 'twas not his fault, and so she said. A mental aberration caused by horse's kick when being forced to unclean stall.

Rosie   Tell him about the randy king before he tells us.

James (*quietly*)   No.

Edmund   The mental aberration, aforesaid, did manifest its lunacy by latching on to accident my mother had. For she did once, attending a tea-party of the King, a tiny slip when curtsying.

Rosie (*incredulous*)   The lies!

Edmund   'Twas but a moment's totter from the combinated cause of hem of skirt and over-zeal, confronted by the awesome right divine. As you can see, and so she said, 'twas but a trifling-totter, but enough to make a mole-hill from the late, lamented, mountain brain of James.

Rosie   Too late.

James (*quietly*)   No.

Edmund   And so, farewell.

Anastasia   Our memories will visit you.

Edmund (*leading* **Anastasia** *away*)   To the sun!

James *withdraws sword from stick.*

James   Thou monstrous faux-pas!

Edmund   What's this?

James   You're going nowhere any more. The crow has come for you. Defend yourself if you like; it's all the same to me.

Edmund   It cannot be helped.

Anastasia   Then be not too severe.

They come together to cross swords.

Edmund   And another thing I know, my brother James was no swordsman.

James   Prepare yourself for a fencing lesson, and for death.

They sword-fight. **Edmund** *looks expert.* **James**' *knowledge of swordplay comes from films about pirates, but even this degree of*

finesse soon deserts him. The fight grows abandoned and bizarre,
James *going through a series of mishaps, pathetic, ridiculous, his*
desperation increasing until, eventually, he starts to roar in
frustration and charges at **Edmund**, *both hands flailing, wielding*
sword-stick and its wooden scabbard. **Edmund** *is thrown by*
James' *total abandon and he loses his sword. The point of*
James' *blade is at* **Edmund**'s *neck.* **James** *hesitates.*
Edmund *is smiling confidently.*

Rosie   Kill him!

This sort of victory is not good enough for **James**. *He drops his*
sword, pretending he is unable to kill **Edmund**. *Then he walks*
away, his hand covering his eyes, as if he were crying. A glance
backward to see if **Edmund** *is following him.* **Edmund** *comes to*
James, *embraces him, warmly.*

Edmund   Now I know who you are.

Still embracing, **James** *withdraws his knife from under his coat,*
and as he stabs **Edmund** *in the back —*

James   Now you can be sure of it.

Edmund, *dying, falls behind the trees.* **James** *starts to cry.*
Anastasia *hurries to help* **Edmund**. **Rosie** *takes* **Edmund**'s
sword, follows, and kills **Anastasia**. **Rosie** *joins* **James**. *Both*
crying through the following.

Rosie   We done it, James.

James   We did.

Rosie   . . . What have we done?

James   . . . We'll see.

Rosie   . . . It's nice to cry, James.

James   . . . Don't be fooled by it, Rosie.

Rosie   . . . You can't trust it, James.

James   . . . We might be laughing in a minute.

They exit crying.